# Science Revision Notes
# For Junior Certificate

## *SHEA MULLALLY*

GILL & MACMILLAN

Gill & Macmillan Ltd
Goldenbridge
Dublin 8
with associated companies throughout the world
© Shea Mullally 1996
0 7171 2256 5
Print origination in Ireland by Typeform Repro Ltd, Dublin

# CONTENTS

## APPLIED SCIENCE

# THE PERIODIC TABLE

## Group

| Period | 1 | 2 | | | | | | | d Block | | | | | | | 3 | 4 | 5 | 6 | 7 | 0 |
|---|---|---|---|---|---|---|---|---|---|---|---|---|---|---|---|---|---|---|---|---|---|
| | | | | | | | | | | | | | | | | | | | | | 2<br>He<br>Helium<br>4.0 |
| **1** | 1<br>H<br>Hydrogen<br>1.0 | | | | | | | | | | | | | | | | | | | | |
| **2** | 3<br>Li<br>Lithium<br>6.9 | 4<br>Be<br>Beryllium<br>9.0 | | | | | | | | | | | | | | 5<br>B<br>Boron<br>10.8 | 6<br>C<br>Carbon<br>12.0 | 7<br>N<br>Nitrogen<br>14.0 | 8<br>O<br>Oxygen<br>16.0 | 9<br>F<br>Fluorine<br>19.0 | 10<br>Ne<br>Neon<br>20.2 |
| **3** | 11<br>Na<br>Sodium<br>23.0 | 12<br>Mg<br>Magnesium<br>24.3 | | | | | | | | | | | | | | 13<br>Al<br>Aluminium<br>27.0 | 14<br>Si<br>Silicon<br>28.1 | 15<br>P<br>Phosphorus<br>31.0 | 16<br>S<br>Sulphur<br>32.1 | 17<br>Cl<br>Chlorine<br>35.5 | 18<br>Ar<br>Argon<br>39.9 |
| **4** | 19<br>K<br>Potassium<br>39.1 | 20<br>Ca<br>Calcium<br>40.1 | 21<br>Sc<br>Scandium<br>45.0 | 22<br>Ti<br>Titanium<br>47.9 | 23<br>V<br>Vanadium<br>50.9 | 24<br>Cr<br>Chromium<br>52.0 | 25<br>Mn<br>Manganese<br>54.9 | 26<br>Fe<br>Iron<br>55.9 | 27<br>Co<br>Cobalt<br>58.9 | 28<br>Ni<br>Nickel<br>58.7 | 29<br>Cu<br>Copper<br>63.5 | 30<br>Zn<br>Zinc<br>65.4 | 31<br>Ga<br>Gallium<br>69.7 | 32<br>Ge<br>Germanium<br>72.6 | 33<br>As<br>Arsenic<br>74.9 | 34<br>Se<br>Selenium<br>79.0 | 35<br>Br<br>Bromine<br>79.9 | 36<br>Kr<br>Krypton<br>83.8 |
| **5** | 37<br>Rb<br>Rubidium<br>85.5 | 38<br>Sr<br>Strontium<br>87.6 | 39<br>Y<br>Yttrium<br>88.9 | 40<br>Zr<br>Zirconium<br>91.2 | 41<br>Nb<br>Niobium<br>92.9 | 42<br>Mo<br>Molybdenum<br>95.9 | 43<br>Tc<br>Technetium<br>(99) | 44<br>Ru<br>Ruthenium<br>101.1 | 45<br>Rh<br>Rhodium<br>102.9 | 46<br>Pd<br>Palladium<br>106.4 | 47<br>Ag<br>Silver<br>107.9 | 48<br>Cd<br>Cadmium<br>112.4 | 49<br>In<br>Indium<br>114.8 | 50<br>Sn<br>Tin<br>118.7 | 51<br>Sb<br>Antimony<br>121.8 | 52<br>Te<br>Tellurium<br>127.6 | 53<br>I<br>Iodine<br>126.9 | 54<br>Xe<br>Xenon<br>131.3 |
| **6** | 55<br>Cs<br>Caesium<br>132.9 | 56<br>Ba<br>Barium<br>137.3 | 57<br>La<br>Lanthanum<br>138.9 | 72<br>Hf<br>Hafnium<br>178.5 | 73<br>Ta<br>Tantalum<br>181.0 | 74<br>W<br>Tungsten<br>183.9 | 75<br>Re<br>Rhenium<br>186.2 | 76<br>Os<br>Osmium<br>190.2 | 77<br>Ir<br>Iridium<br>192.2 | 78<br>Pt<br>Platinum<br>195.1 | 79<br>Au<br>Gold<br>197.0 | 80<br>Hg<br>Mercury<br>200.6 | 81<br>Tl<br>Thallium<br>204.4 | 82<br>Pb<br>Lead<br>207.2 | 83<br>Bi<br>Bismuth<br>209.0 | 84<br>Po<br>Polonium<br>(210) | 85<br>At<br>Astatine<br>(210) | 86<br>Rn<br>Radon<br>(222) |
| **7** | 87<br>Fr<br>Francium<br>(223) | 88<br>Ra<br>Radium<br>(226) | 87<br>Ac<br>Actinium<br>(227) | 104<br>Unq<br>Unnil-<br>quadium<br>(261) | 105<br>Unp<br>Unnil-<br>pentium<br>(262) | 106<br>Unh<br>Unnil-<br>hexium<br>(263) | | | | | | | | | | | | |

**Key**

| Atomic number |
| Symbol |
| Name |
| Relative atomic Mass |

# PHYSICS

## CHAPTER 1. MATTER, MEASUREMENT AND ENERGY

## WHAT IS PHYSICS?

Physics is the study of the physical properties of substances. It involves the measurement of matter and energy.

## MATTER

Matter is anything that has mass and which takes up space.

Matter can exist in three forms or states: solids, liquids and gases.

Matter is interchangeable, i.e. water is a liquid, but at high temperatures it becomes steam, which is a gas. At low temperatures water becomes ice, which is a solid.

| **Solid** | ⇔ | **Liquid** | ⇔ | **Gas** |
|-----------|---|------------|---|---------|
| Ice | ⇔ | Water | ⇔ | Steam |

| Property | Solid | Liquid | Gas |
|----------|-------|--------|-----|
| Attractive forces | Strong | Weak | Very weak |
| Shape | Definite | Not definite, depends on container | Not definite, fills any container |
| Volume | Definite | Definite | Not definite |
| Mobility | Fixed, but can vibrate | Able to flow | Completely free movement |

## MEASUREMENT

The most important quantities measured in physics are **length, mass and time**. All other measurable quantities are related to these.

### Instruments used in measurement

- **Opisometer** measures curved lines.
- **Vernier calipers** measures the thickness or the diameter of a substance.
- **Weighing scales** (laboratory balance) measures the mass of a substance.
- **Pendulum** measures time. The time of the swing depends on the length of the pendulum.

- **Graduated cylinder** measures the volume of a liquid. It can also be used to measure the volume of irregular solids.

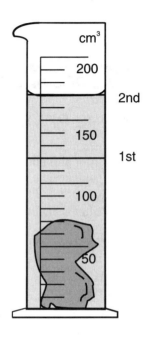

### Units and symbols used in measurement

| Quantity | Unit | Symbol | Other Units used |
|----------|------|--------|------------------|
| Length | metre | m | kilometre (km), centimetre (cm), millimetre (mm) |
| Mass | gram | g | kilogram (kg) |
| Time | second | s | minute, hour |
| Area | square metre | $m^2$ | square centimetre ($cm^2$) |
| Volume | cubic metre | $m^3$ | cubic centimetre ($cm^3$), litre (l) |

## ENERGY

When something has energy it is capable of doing work. **Energy is the ability to do work**. It is measured in joules (J).

### Different types of energy

- **Kinetic energy** is the energy an object has when it is moving.

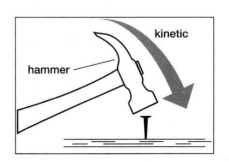

- **Potential energy** is stored energy waiting to do work.
- **Chemical energy** is stored energy in oil, gas, coal and all other chemicals, waiting to react.
- **Nuclear energy** is stored energy in radioactive substances. It is used in power stations to generate electricity.
- **Electrical energy** is one of the most useful forms of energy. It can be used in many forms, including heat, light and sound.
- **Heat energy** is in all objects at a temperature above zero Kelvin. Heat energy is generated because of particle movement: the greater the movement, the greater the heat energy released.
- **Light energy** travels in waves. The energy from the sun takes the form of light and heat energy.
- **Sound energy** travels in waves. Sound causes our ear-drums to vibrate, enabling us to distinguish different sounds.

potential energy

*Energy conversions*

**The law of conservation of energy: energy cannot be created or destroyed, but can only be changed from one form into another.**

The following are some examples of energy conversions.

| Instrument | Energy in | Energy out |
|---|---|---|
| Coiled spring | Potential | Kinetic |
| Generator | Kinetic | Electrical |
| Motor | Electrical | Kinetic |
| Battery | Chemical | Electrical |
| Car | Chemical | Kinetic |
| Microphone | Sound | Electrical |
| Bulb | Electrical | Light |

*Energy supplies and needs*

Many energy conversions are needed in everyday life, e.g. in cooking, heating, and for electrical appliances such as computers and television sets.

Energy comes from **non-renewable sources**, such as coal, gas and other fossil fuels. This energy may be used up some day.

Energy also comes from **renewable sources**, such as solar energy (from the sun), wind energy, wave energy, geothermal energy (from the earth) and hydroelectric energy (from water).

### Saving energy

Energy can be saved by:
- more efficient insulation of homes and factories
- increasing the efficiency of machines
- reusing and recycling materials.

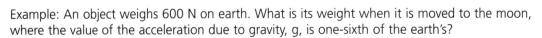

**CHAPTER 2. MASS, DENSITY AND MOTION**

# MASS

All matter, whether it is a solid, a liquid or a gas has mass.

**Mass is the amount of matter in a substance.** It is measured in kilograms (kg).

## WEIGHT

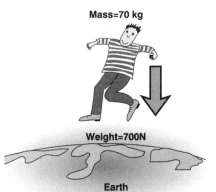

Mass=70 kg

**Weight is the gravitational force from the earth.**
It is measured in newtons (N).

**Mass and weight are related by the force of gravity.**

**weight = mass x g**
(where g is the gravitational force = 10 N/kg)
weight  =  mass x 10 N/kg
        =  70 kg x 10 N/kg
        =  700 N

**Weight=700N**

**Earth**

i.e. a person with a mass of 70 kg weighs 700 N

Example: An object weighs 600 N on earth. What is its weight when it is moved to the moon, where the value of the acceleration due to gravity, g, is one-sixth of the earth's?

Weight on moon   =   $\dfrac{\text{weight on earth}}{6}$

            =   $\dfrac{600\text{ N}}{6}$  =  100 N

# DENSITY

Is steel heavier than wood? The answer to this question depends on the quantities of steel and wood. If we compare equal volumes of steel and wood, we find that steel has more mass than wood, i.e. it is more dense.

$$\textbf{density} \ = \ \frac{\textbf{mass}}{\textbf{volume}}$$

Example: A stone has a mass of 40 g and a volume of 10 cm³. What is its density?

$$\text{density} \ = \ \frac{\text{mass}}{\text{volume}} \ = \ \frac{40 \text{ g}}{10 \text{ cm}^3} \ = \ 4 \text{ g/cm}^3 \ ( \text{ or g cm}^{-3} )$$

## *Density of regular-shaped objects*

1. Find the mass of the wooden block using a balance.
   mass = 12 g
2. Measure the length, width and height. Calculate the volume using the formula:
   V   = l x w x h.
   V   = 4 cm x 3 cm x 2 cm
   V   = 24 cm³

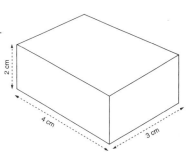

3. Density $= \dfrac{\text{mass}}{\text{volume}} = \dfrac{12 \text{ g}}{24 \text{ cm}^3} = 0.5 \text{ g cm}^{-3}$

## *Density of irregular-shaped objects*

1. Find the mass of the stone using a balance.
2. Measure the rise in volume of the water when the stone is lowered carefully into the water: the rise in volume is the volume of the stone.
3. Density $= \dfrac{\text{mass}}{\text{volume}}$

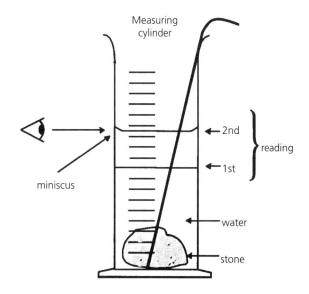

Measuring cylinder

←2nd ⎫
      ⎬ reading
←1st  ⎭

miniscus

water

stone

## Volume of liquids

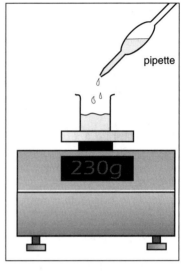

pipette

1. Find the mass of an empty beaker using a balance.
2. Using a pipette, place 100 cm³ of liquid in the beaker.
3. Find the mass of the beaker plus the liquid.
4. Subtract the mass of the beaker from this to find the mass of the liquid.
5. Density $= \dfrac{\text{mass}}{\text{volume}}$

### Flotation and density

Cork is less dense than water, so it floats. Copper is more dense than water, so it sinks.

**A body will float in a liquid if it is less dense than the liquid.**

## MOTION: SPEED, VELOCITY AND ACCELERATION

### Speed
**Speed is the rate of change of distance with time.**

The world's fastest athletes can run 100 m in 10 seconds. The average speed of the athlete is found by dividing the distance travelled by the amount of time taken.

$$\textbf{speed} = \frac{\textbf{distance}}{\textbf{time}} = \frac{100 \text{ m}}{10 \text{ s}} = 10 \text{ m/s (or 10 m s}^{-1})$$

### Velocity
**Velocity is speed in a given direction.**

Like speed, velocity is measured in metres per second (m/s). It tells us the speed that something is travelling, and also the direction in which it is travelling, e.g. an athlete is running with a velocity of 7 m/s due south.

**Distance/time graphs** are used to calculate velocity.

When an object is **stationary** the distance travelled does not change with time.
Therefore, velocity = 0 m/s.

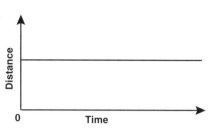

When an object is moving at **constant velocity** the speed remains the same.

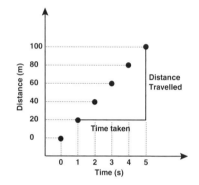

| Time(s) | 0 | 1 | 2 | 3 | 4 | 5 |
|---|---|---|---|---|---|---|
| Distance (m) | 0 | 20 | 40 | 60 | 80 | 100 |

$$\textbf{velocity} \; = \; \frac{\textbf{distance}}{\textbf{time}} \; = \; \frac{100\ m}{5\ s} \; = \; 20\ m/s \quad (or\ 20\ m\ s^{-1})$$

## Acceleration

**Acceleration is the change in velocity divided by the time taken.**

When an object increases its velocity, it is accelerating. When it decreases its velocity, it is decelerating.

Example: A car takes 10 seconds to change its velocity from 20 m/s to 50 m/s. What is its acceleration?

$$\textbf{acceleration} \; = \; \frac{\textbf{change in velocity}}{\textbf{time taken}} \; = \; \frac{50\ m/s \; - \; 20\ m/s}{10\ s} \; = \; \frac{30\ m/s}{10\ s}$$

$$= \; 3\ m/s/s$$

The car has an acceleration of 3 metres per second per second (3 m/s/s). This is usually written as 3 m/s$^2$ or as 3 m s$^{-2}$.

Example: A car starts from rest with a constant acceleration of 5 m s$^{-2}$. How long will it take to reach a speed of 30 m s$^{-1}$?

$$\textbf{Acceleration} \quad = \quad \frac{\textbf{change in velocity}}{\textbf{time taken}}$$

$$5 \text{ m s}^{-2} \quad = \quad \frac{30 \text{ m s}^{-1} - 0}{t}$$

$$t \quad = \quad \frac{30 \text{ m s}^{-1}}{5 \text{ m s}^{-2}} \quad = 6 \text{ seconds}$$

**Velocity/time graphs** are used to calculate acceleration.

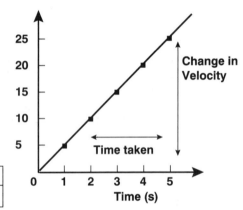

| Time(s)        | 0 | 1 | 2  | 3  | 4  | 5  |
|----------------|---|---|----|----|----|----|
| Velocity (m/s) | 0 | 5 | 10 | 15 | 20 | 25 |

The object is accelerating at 5 m/s/s (5 m s$^{-2}$).

# FORCES

**A force is anything that tries to change the shape, the direction or the velocity of a body.**

There are many different kinds of force: pushing, pulling, bending, squeezing, twisting, stretching etc.

One of the most important forces is the pull of gravity, which we call weight. **Force is measured in newtons (N).**

## Pairs of forces: action and reaction

**For every force there is an equal and opposite reaction.**

No force can act on its own. When a bullet is fired from a rifle, the rifle recoils.

This shows that forces always occur in pairs.

## Momentum

A small car which is travelling very fast and which hits a wall, can cause as much damage to the wall as a large bus which is travelling slowly. In both cases it is the momentum of the object that does the damage.

mass  8000 kg
speed 10 m/s
momentum 80 000 kg m/s

mass 1000 kg
speed 80 m/s
momentum 80 000 kg m/s

**Momentum of an object  =  mass  x  velocity**

## Friction

When two objects come into contact with each other they experience a force known as friction. Rubbing your hands together, sliding on ice, and scraping paint off glass are all examples of friction.

**Friction is a force which stops things sliding over each other.**

Friction is used to slow down motor cars when the brakes come into contact with the wheels. Friction is reduced in cars by designing them to resist air flow.

## LEVERS

A door, a wheelbarrow, a see-saw and a spanner are all examples of levers. Levers make it easier to turn and twist things.

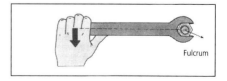

**A lever is any rigid body which is free to turn about a fixed point called a fulcrum.**

## Moment of a force

Sometimes when we apply a force, it causes an object to turn or twist, e.g. opening a bottle or turning a nut with a spanner. The turning effect of a force is called a **moment.**

**moment = force applied x perpendicular distance of force from the fulcrum**

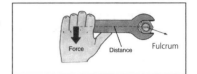

moment = force x distance =
500 N x 2 m = 1000 Nm (small moment)

moment = force x distance =
1000 N x 4 m = 4000 Nm (larger moment)

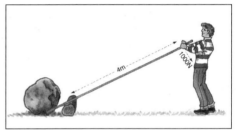

## Balancing moments

Objects are balanced when the moments of the forces acting on them are balanced.

**When an object is balanced the moments on the left equal the moments on the right.**

**20 x 30 = 15 x 40**
**600 = 600**

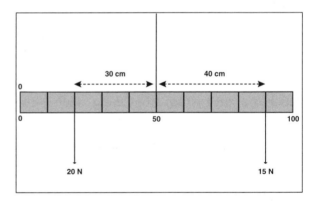

## Levers at equilibrium

***Law of the lever: when a lever is balanced, the sum of the moments on the left equals the sum of the moments on the right.***

The lever in the diagram is balanced under the action of the forces shown. Find the value of W.

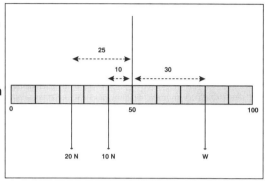

| moments on left | = | moments on right |
|---|---|---|
| $(20 \times 25) + (10 \times 10)$ | = | $W \times 30$ |
| $500 + 100$ | = | $30 \times W$ |
| $W$ | = | $20$ N |

## Centre of gravity

In the previous diagram, the metre stick was suspended at the mid-point. This point is where the weight appears to act. **The centre of gravity of an object is the point where all its weight appears to act.**

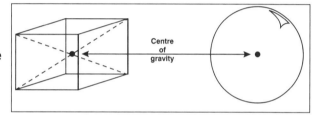

### Finding the centre of gravity of a sheet of cardboard

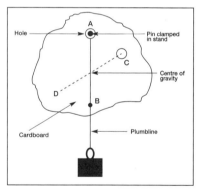

1. Hang the cardboard from a pin on a stand. Make sure that it is free to swing about.
2. When the cardboard comes to rest, draw a vertical line on the cardboard along the plumbline.
3. Hang the cardboard from a different position and repeat step 2.
4. The centre of gravity is the point where the two lines cross.

## Stability

When buildings are designed, great care is taken to ensure that they do not topple over, i.e. that they are in stable equilibrium. This is done by making sure that each building has a wide base and that the centre of gravity is as low as possible.

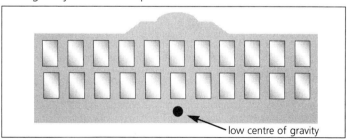

low centre of gravity

### Stable, unstable and neutral equilibrium

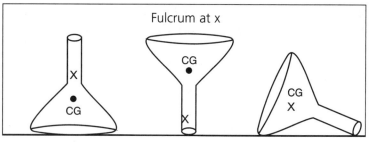

Fulcrum at x

- **Stable** equilibrium occurs when the fulcrum is above the centre of gravity.
- **Unstable** equilibrium occurs when the fulcrum is below the centre of gravity.
- **Neutral** equilibrium occurs when the fulcrum is at the centre of gravity.

## *Work*

Work is done and energy is used when a body is moved.

## work done  =  force  x  distance moved

**The unit of work is the joule (J).** 1 joule of work is done when a force of 1 newton moves a body 1 metre.

Example: What is the work done when a brick of mass 3 kg is lifted through a vertical height of 2 metres?

work done  =  force  x  distance moved
work done  =  30 N  x  2 m  ⇐  **3 kg  =  30 N**
       =  60 Nm
       =  60 J

---

## CHAPTER 4. PRESSURE

The effect of a force on a substance depends on how the force is spread out over the surface of the substance.

The two women in the diagram have the same weight. The woman with the stiletto heels can cause damage to the floor covering, because her weight is concentrated over a small area. Because her weight is spread over a small area it produces high pressure, while the weight of the other woman spread over a large area produces low pressure.

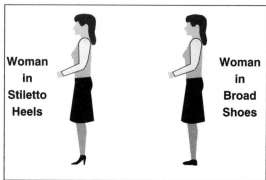

Woman
in
Stiletto
Heels

Woman
in
Broad
Shoes

$$\textbf{pressure} = \frac{\textbf{force}}{\textbf{area}}$$

**Pressure is force per unit area.**

Pressure is measured in **pascals**: **1 pascal (Pa)** = **1 N/m$^2$ (or 1Nm$^{-2}$)**

Example: The weight of the block is 600 N. Find the smallest pressure it can exert on the surface.

### Surface A

**area of surface A** = 3 m x 2 m = 6 m$^2$

$$\textbf{pressure} = \frac{\textbf{force}}{\textbf{area}}$$

$$= \frac{600\ N}{6\ m^2} = 100\ N/m^2\ (or\ 100\ N\ m^{-2})$$

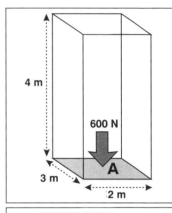

### Surface B

**area of surface B** = 4 m x 2 m = 8 m$^2$

$$\textbf{pressure} = \frac{\textbf{force}}{\textbf{area}}$$

$$= \frac{600\ N}{8\ m^2} = 75\ N/m^2\ (or\ 75\ N\ m^{-2})$$

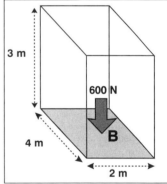

### Surface C

**area of surface C** = 3 m x 4 m = 12 m$^2$

$$\textbf{pressure} = \frac{\textbf{force}}{\textbf{area}}$$

$$= \frac{600\ N}{12\ m^2} = 50\ N/m^2\ (or\ 50\ N\ m^{-2})$$

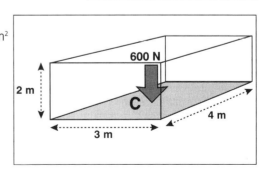

Therefore, the smallest pressure is exerted by surface C.

### Pressure in fluids (liquids and gases)

When underwater, a diver experiences pressure from the liquid all around him. The deeper he dives the greater is the pressure exerted.

**The pressure in a liquid depends on the height of the liquid above and on the density of the liquid.**

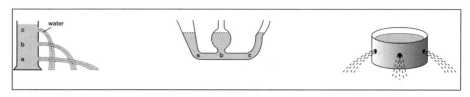

- Pressure increases with depth
- Width or shape do not affect pressure.
- The pressure in a liquid is the same in all directions.

### Hydraulic pressure

Liquids are very difficult to compress. If a small force is applied to a liquid (using piston A), it will create an equal pressure throughout the liquid. If this pressure is passed on to the other side of the container, it will create a larger upwards force on

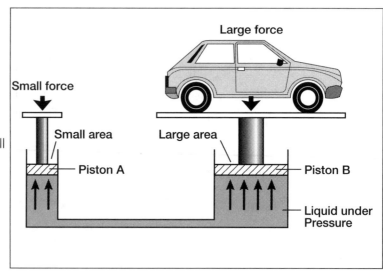

piston B, because piston B has a larger area. This allows the hydraulic jack to lift up the car.

## *Atmospheric pressure*

Air is a fluid and exerts pressure in the same way that water does.

## Air exerts pressure.

1. Boil a small amount of water in a metal can until the air is driven out.
2. Remove the heat and quickly seal the can.
3. Cool the can by pouring some water over it.
4. After a while, the can will collapse under the atmospheric pressure.

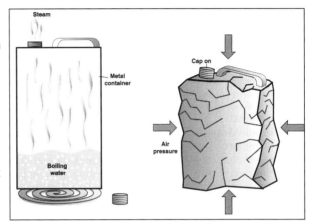

## Other effects

Atmospheric pressure holds the card in place.

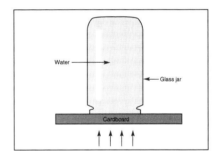

Rubber suckers are held on by atmospheric pressure.

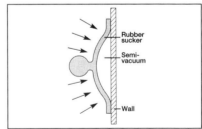

When the air is sucked out, atmospheric pressure pushes up the liquid.

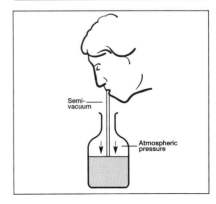

### *Measuring atmospheric pressure*

An instrument called a **barometer** is used to measure atmospheric pressure.

### Mercury barometer

Atmospheric pressure holds up the column of mercury. Normal atmospheric pressure holds up a column of 76 cm of mercury. The height of the column is measured from the top of the mercury to the surface of the mercury in the dish.

When atmospheric pressure increases, the mercury rises slightly up the tube. When atmospheric pressure decreases, the mercury falls slightly down the tube.

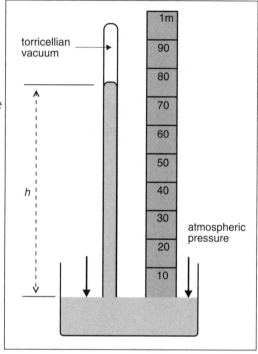

### Aneroid barometer (no liquid)

An aneroid barometer is made of a partially evacuated corrugated box. If atmospheric pressure increases, the box is crushed slightly, causing the pointer to move. When the pressure decreases, the pointer moves the other way.

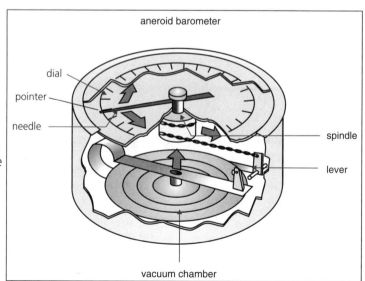

### Altitude and pressure

The greater the height above sea-level, the less the atmospheric pressure becomes. An instrument called an **altimeter** is used by pilots to measure height above sea-level. It does this by measuring the pressure on a barometer.

### Weather and pressure

When the atmospheric pressure is high, water vapour does not rise from the ground. This means that rain clouds do not form and the weather is fine and sunny.

When the atmospheric pressure is low, water vapour rises up from the ground. Rain clouds form which may cause rain.

### Water and pressure

Increase in pressure increases the boiling point of water and decreases the freezing point of water.

## CHAPTER 5. HEAT AND TEMPERATURE

# HEAT

Heat is a form of energy.  It can cause movement of particles and can be converted into other forms of energy.

### Heat movement

Heat can move from a hot region to a cold region in three ways: by conduction, by convection and by radiation.

**Conduction is the movement of heat through a substance without the substance moving.**

When a metal bar is heated at one end the particles at that end start to vibrate. The vibrations are passed along the bar from one particle to the next. In this way heat is transferred to the other end of the bar.

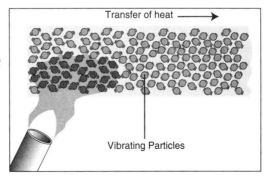

Transfer of heat ⟶

Vibrating Particles

## Metals are good conductors

1. Pour boiling water into the container.
2. The small nail under the wax will fall from the copper first, showing that copper is a good conductor
3. The small nail will not fall from the glass, showing that glass, a non-metal, is a poor conductor.
4. The nail then falls off the other metals.

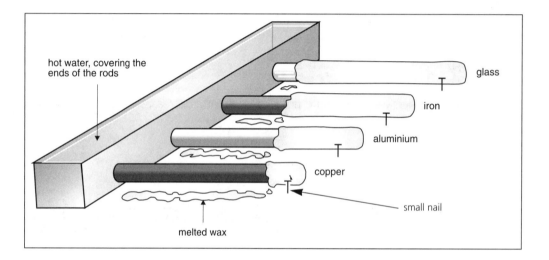

hot water, covering the ends of the rods

glass

iron

aluminium

copper

small nail

melted wax

## Water is a poor conductor

1. Heat the water at the top of the test-tube.
2. The water at the top boils; the ice at the bottom does not melt.
3. This shows that water is a poor conductor of heat.

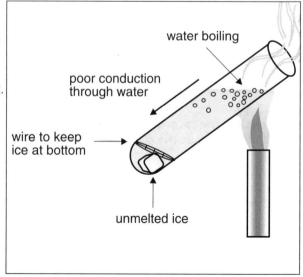

water boiling

poor conduction through water

wire to keep ice at bottom

unmelted ice

**Insulation: An insulator is a substance which does not allow heat to move through it easily.**

Non-metals, such as wood, wool and glass, liquids and gases are good insulators (or bad conductors).

The insulating ability of a material is given by its **tog value**. The higher the tog value, the better the insulator.

**Convection is the movement of heat through liquids and gases**.

The particles in the liquid or gas move and carry the heat from one place to another.

**Convection currents in water**
1. Place some cold water in a beaker.
2. Drop a crystal of potassium permanganate down a funnel into a corner of the beaker.
3. Heat the water gently just below the crystal.
4. The water molecules near the crystal rise up and are replaced by cold water molecules. Purple convection currents are seen moving through the water.

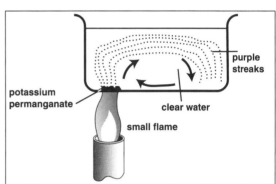

**Radiation is the transfer of heat, in rays, from a hot body without needing a medium to travel through.** The radiation travels in straight lines at the speed of light.

**Dark surfaces radiate heat better than bright surfaces**
1. Find two cans of equal size: one polished and shiny, the other dull and black.
2. Put a thermometer in each can and fill each can with equal amounts of boiling water.
3. Cover each can. Record the temperature every 2 minutes.
4. The temperature falls more quickly in the darker can.

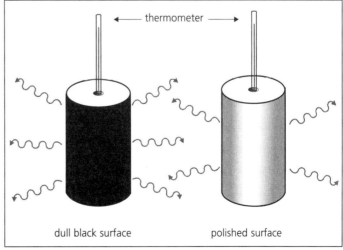

**Dark surfaces absorb heat better than bright surfaces**

1. Find two cans of equal size: one polished and shiny, the other dull and black.
2. Put a thermometer in each can and fill each can with **equal amounts** of cold water.
3. Place each can an **equal distance** from a strongly glowing electric heater. Record the temperature every 2 minutes.
4. The temperature rises more quickly in the darker can.

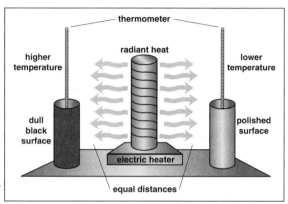

# EXPANSION AND CONTRACTION

Solids, liquids and gases expand when they are heated and contract when they are cooled.

Substances expand when they are heated because the particles vibrate more quickly and take up more space.

Gases expand more than liquids, while liquids expand more than solids.

## *Expansion of solids, liquids and gases*

Expansion of solids:

The cold ball slips through the ring. When it is heated strongly it expands and will not fit through the ring.

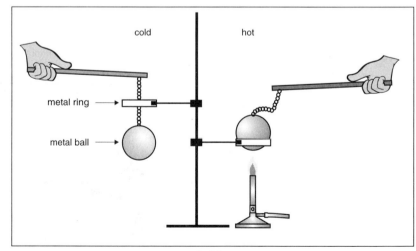

Solid

20

Expansion of liquids:

When the flask is put into a beaker of hot water, the water-level in the capillary tube rises.

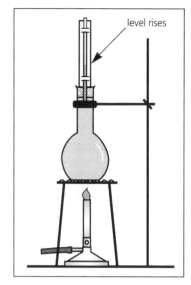

Liquid

Expansion of gases:

The heat from your hand expands the air in the test-tube.
This is seen as air bubbles rising from the water in the beaker.

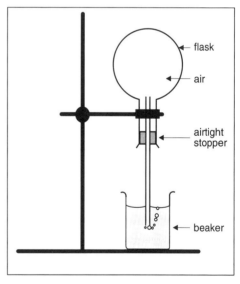

Gas

### The bimetallic strip

Different substances expand by different amounts when heated. When the bimetallic strip is heated, the copper expands more than the steel, causing the strip to bend. When the strip is cooled it straightens out again.

Bimetallic strips are used as **thermostats** in electric fires, electric kettles, fridges and washing machines. Thermostats keep the temperature at a steady level.

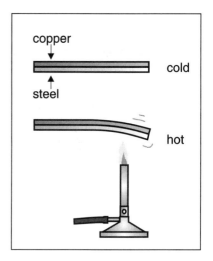

### Temperature

**Temperature is the measure of hotness or coldness of a body.**

Temperature is usually measured in degrees Celsius or °C using a thermometer.

Mercury thermometers

- expand easily when heated
- have high boiling points
- do not wet the glass
- are expensive.

Alcohol thermometers

- are sensitive to small changes
- must be coloured
- wet the glass
- are cheap.

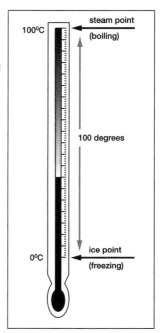

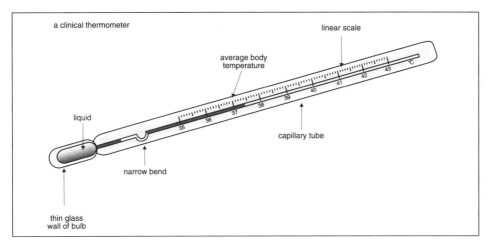

Clinical thermometers
- are used to measure body temperature
- have a scale that reads from 34 °C to 43 °C.
  They are very accurate over this range.
- have a constriction that prevents the mercury returning to the bulb, allowing plenty of time to take someone's temperature.

### Heat and temperature

1. The temperature of the water in both beakers is the same.
2. The amount of heat in beaker 2 is twice the amount of that in beaker 1.
3. The amount of heat depends not only on the temperature of the substance, but also on the **mass of the substance.**

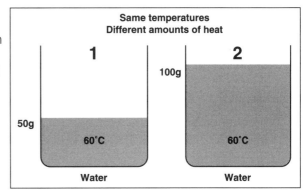

1. The temperature of the liquids in both beakers is the same.
2. The amount of heat in beaker 2 is different to that in beaker 1.
3. The amount of heat depends also on the **nature of the substance**.

**Heat depends on temperature, mass and the nature of the substance.**

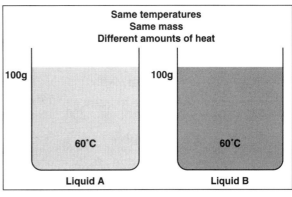

## CHANGES OF STATE

- **Melting and freezing:** When ice receives heat energy it melts. It changes from a solid to a liquid. When water loses heat it freezes and changes into ice.
- **Evaporation and boiling:** When water is heated it evaporates and changes into steam. It changes from a liquid into a gas. Evaporation occurs at the surface of the liquid. When it occurs throughout the liquid, the liquid is at its boiling point. When steam loses heat energy it condenses and changes into water.
- **Latent heat:** The heat taken in without a temperature change during melting and boiling is called latent heat.
- **Changes of state:** There is no change in temperature during a change of state.
- **Pressure:** An increase in pressure raises the boiling point of a substance. A decrease in pressure lowers the melting point of a substance.
- **Sublimation:** Some substances have the ability to change directly from the solid state into the gaseous state when heated. Iodine and ammonium chloride sublime when they are heated.

## CHAPTER 6. WAVE MOTION, SOUND AND LIGHT

# WAVE MOTION

Waves occur in all sorts of ways: water waves, sound waves, light waves, dominoes toppling, shock waves from earthquakes, X-rays, IR radiation and other electromagnetic rays.

**A wave is a means of transferring energy from one place to another.**

### Properties of waves

**Wavelength** is the distance from one crest to the next. It is measured in metres.

**Frequency** is the number of waves passing a fixed point per second. It is measured in hertz (Hz or s⁻¹).

**Amplitude** is the maximum displacement of the wave from a rest position. This is shown as the height of the wave from the centre line.

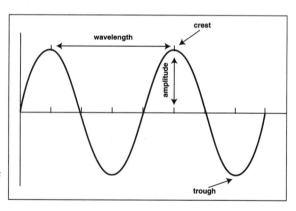

### Wave equation:
$$\text{velocity} = \text{wavelength} \times \text{frequency}$$
$$V = \lambda f$$

Example: A wave has a frequency of 220 Hz and a velocity of 330 m s⁻¹. What is its wavelength?

$V = \lambda f$ *(Remember 1 Hz = 1 s⁻¹)*

$330 \text{ ms}^{-1} = \lambda \times 220 \text{ s}^{-1}$

$\lambda = \dfrac{330 \text{ ms}^{-1}}{220 \text{ s}^{-1}} = 1.5 \text{ m}$

### Electromagnetic spectrum

Light waves, radio waves, microwaves, UV and IR are all part of the electromagnetic spectrum. Radio waves are relatively long waves, while gamma rays are relatively very short waves.

## SOUND

### Sound is a form of energy.

Place a vibrating tuning fork beside a table tennis ball. The table tennis ball will move.

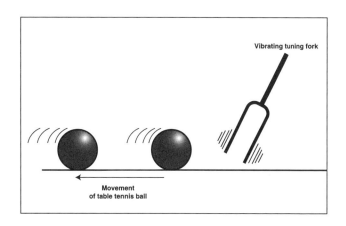

Vibrating tuning fork

Movement
of table tennis ball

### Sound is a wave motion.

Hold a vibrating tuning fork in front of a microphone. A wave pattern will appear on the oscilloscope screen.

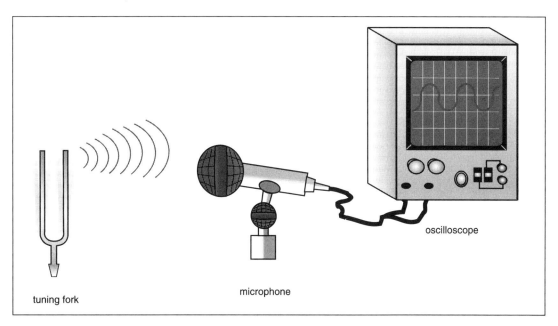

oscilloscope

microphone

tuning fork

## Sound cannot travel through a vacuum.

Allow the bell to ring and, as air is evacuated from the jar, the sound will begin to fade.
When all the air is evacuated no sound is heard, even though the hammer is still striking the gong.

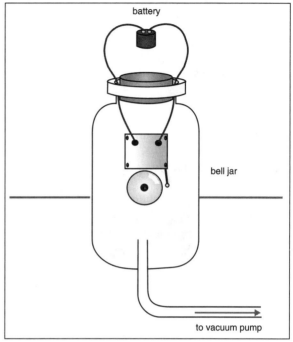

## Sound travels through air at 330 m s⁻¹.

## Sound can be reflected.

Adjust the position of tube B until the ticking of the clock is at its loudest. At this point the angle X is equal to the angle Y.

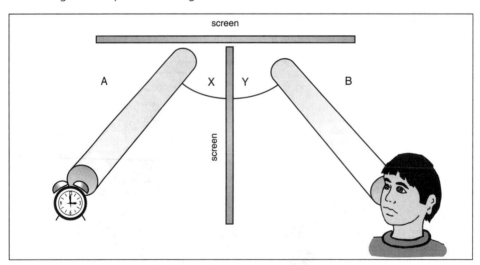

The **loudness** of a sound depends on the amplitude of the sound wave. Loud sounds have large amplitudes.

**Pitch** depends on the frequency, i.e. high pitch depends on high frequency.

**Noise** is a jumble of unrelated waves of different wavelength.

A **musical note** is a regular wave of single wavelength.

# LIGHT

## Light is a form of energy.

Light makes the vanes on the radiometer move.

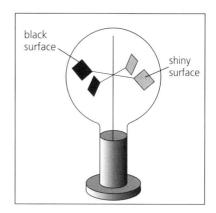

## Light travels in straight lines (rays).

When all the holes are in a straight line, light is seen. When the middle card is moved to one side, light is not seen.

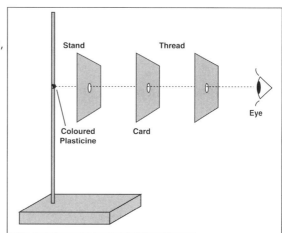

## Light is reflected.

Rays of light from the light box are marked on the paper before and after they hit the mirror. A regular pattern results.

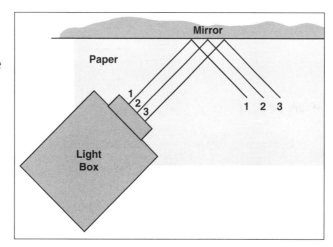

## Light is refracted.

Refraction is the bending of light when it travels from one transparent substance into another.
Light is bent when rays of light pass from one medium to another.

The ruler seems to be broken when it is placed at an angle in the water. This shows that the light rays are bent as they emerge from the water.

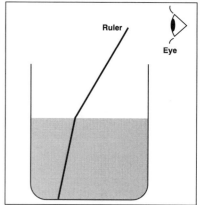

## White light is dispersed by refraction.

Dispersion is the breaking up of white light into different colours.

When a ray of white light enters the prism it is bent and emerges as a band of colours called a spectrum.

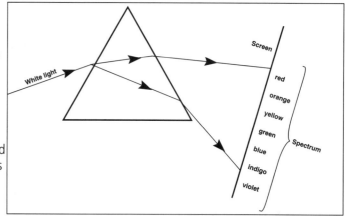

## *Colours of light*

**Primary** colours are red, green and blue.

**Secondary** colours are cyan, yellow and magenta.

**Complementary** colours are a primary colour and a secondary colour that together give white, e.g. blue and yellow, red and cyan, green and magenta.

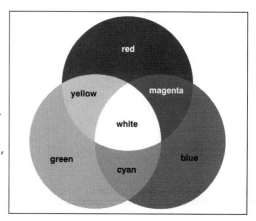

## Lenses

**Convex** lenses are converging lens (come together).

**Concave** lenses are diverging lens (spread out).

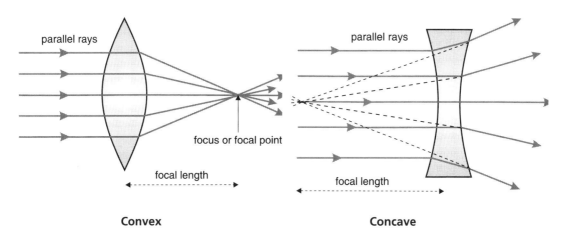

Convex                                         Concave

---

**CHAPTER 7. ELECTRICITY AND MAGNETISM**

# ELECTRICITY

Electricity is a form of energy and may be converted into other forms.

### Simple circuits

Energy is needed to move electrical charges around a circuit. The energy is usually supplied from a **battery**, which is an electrical pump. It pumps electrons from a region of high electrical pressure to a region of low electrical pressure. The difference in electrical pressure is called **potential difference** and is measured in **volts**.

Electricity will flow in the circuit if there is a complete circuit and a potential difference.

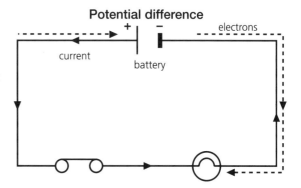

## Electrical conductors and insulators

The substance to be tested is placed between the clips. If the bulb lights the substance is a conductor, if it does not light it is an insulator.

**Conductor**s are substances which allow electricity to flow.
**Insulators** are substances which do not allow electricity to flow.

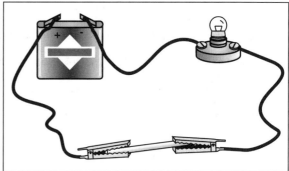

## Series circuits

Bulbs connected in series are connected one after another.

The bulbs light because they resist the flow of electricity through the circuit. The more resistance in a circuit the less current will flow.

As more bulbs are connected the light gets dimmer as the current reduces. If one bulb is disconnected, the circuit is broken.

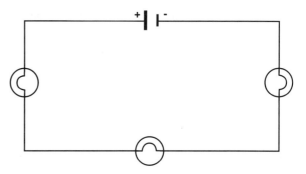

**(a) Series circuit**

## Parallel circuits

Bulbs connected in parallel are connected side by side.

Bulbs are brighter in a parallel circuit. When one bulb is disconnected (or blows), the others continue to glow.

As more bulbs are added, more current is used. This means that the battery runs down more quickly.

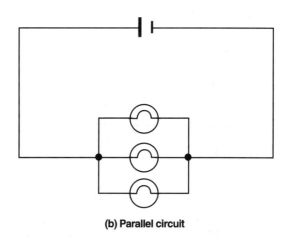

**(b) Parallel circuit**

**Current** is the flow of electric charge. It is measured in **amperes** (A).

**Potential difference (voltage)** is the difference in electrical pressure. It is measured in **volts** (V).

**Resistance** is the ability that a substance has to resist the flow of electricity in a circuit. It is measured in **ohms** ($\Omega$).

## *Symbols for circuits*

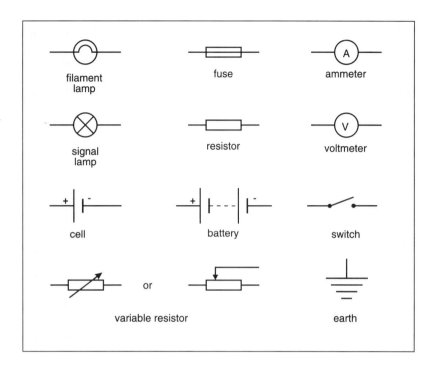

filament lamp

fuse

ammeter

signal lamp

resistor

voltmeter

cell

battery

switch

variable resistor

or

earth

## Ohm's Law: for a conductor at constant temperature,

$$\text{resistance} = \frac{\text{voltage}}{\text{current}} \quad \text{or} \quad R = \frac{V}{I} \quad \text{or} \quad V = I \times R.$$

Example: What is the voltage when a current of 0.5 amps flows through the three resistors connected in series?

Total resistance $\quad \mathbf{R = R_1 + R_2 + R_3}$

$= (3 + 4 + 5)$ ohms

$= 12$ ohms

$\mathbf{V = I \times R}$

$V = 0.5$ amps x 12 ohms

$= 6$ volts

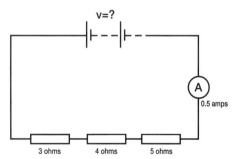

v=?

A
0.5 amps

3 ohms    4 ohms    5 ohms

## Electricity in the home

**Fuses:** When a current exceeds a certain value, the fuse melts and breaks the circuit.

Appliances with 3 amp fuses include televisions, radios, bedside lamps, etc.

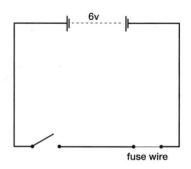

fuse wire

**Plugs:** The live wire is brown and is connected to the fuse; the neutral wire is blue; the earth wire is green and yellow.

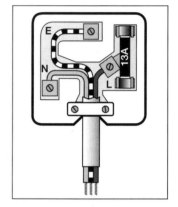

**Lighting circuit:** Lights are connected in parallel. If one light is switched off or blows, the others continue to light.

**Ring main circuit:** The live and neutral wires form a loop or ring. A third loop is formed by the earth wire. No current should flow in the earth wire unless a fault develops.

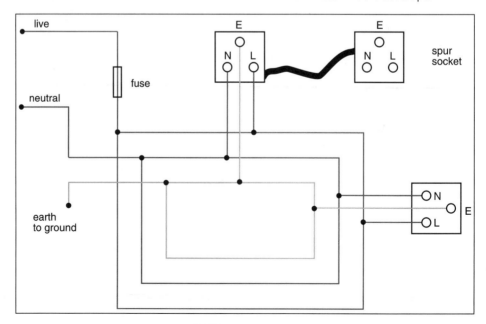

**Power:** Power is measured in watts. The ESB charges a fee for the number of kilowatts used per hour.

kilowatt hours = kilowatts x hours

The number of units of electricity used by a 2 kilowatt heater in 5 hours

= 2 kilowatt x 5 hours = 10 kilowatt hours = 10 units.

**Cost:** The cost of using 5 x100 watts for 12 hours at a cost of 8p per unit

= 5 x 0.1 x 12 x 8 p = 48 p.

## Effects of electricity

**Heating effect:** The filament heats up and the bulb lights.

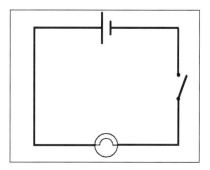

**Magnetic effect:** The compass needle deflects, showing that there is a magnetic field around the wire.

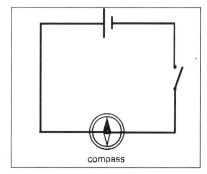

compass

**Chemical effect:**
Bubbles of hydrogen are seen at one electrode and bubbles of oxygen are seen rising at the other electrode. Twice as much hydrogen as oxygen is produced. This occurs because water ($H_2O$) contains two hydrogens and one oxygen

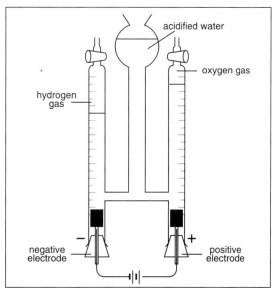

acidified water

oxygen gas

hydrogen gas

negative electrode

positive electrode

## Static electricity

**Static electricity is non-moving electricity.**

**Static electricity is produced by friction.** If you comb your hair and then hold the comb close to a small piece of paper, the piece of paper will probably stick to the comb.

**Electrons have a negative charge.**
Electrons are transferred by friction during the rubbing process from one object to the other.

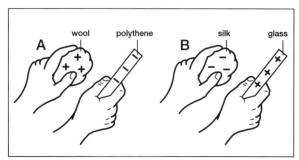

A body is **negatively** charged when it **gains electrons**.

A body is **positively** charged when it **loses electrons**.

**Unlike charges attract** each other.

**Like charges repel** each other.

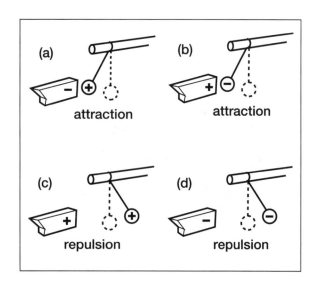

Thunder and lightning are caused by static electricity between clouds.

Photocopiers, dust precipitators, paint and crop sprays use static electricity.

# MAGNETISM

Substances that can be magnetised are **iron, steel, nickel and cobalt.**

**Magnetic poles:** Like poles repel, unlike poles attract.

The space around which a magnet exerts a force is called its **magnetic field**.

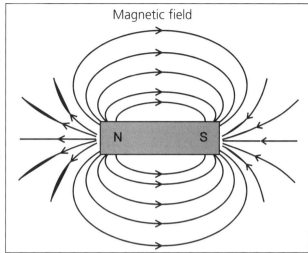

Magnetic field

## *Magnetic field around a bar magnet*

Place a glass (or cardboard) over the bar magnet. Sprinkle iron filings on the glass, then tap gently. The lines of forces are seen.

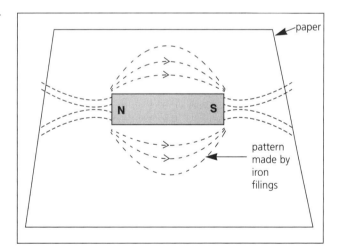

paper

pattern made by iron filings

## Magnetic field around a straight wire

Sprinkle the iron filings on the cardboard then tap gently. The lines of force are seen as circles. The direction is indicated by the right-hand grip rule.

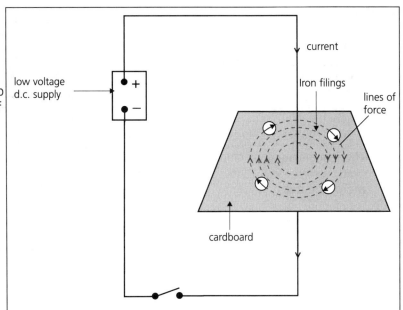

current

low voltage d.c. supply

Iron filings

lines of force

cardboard

## Magnetic field due to a solenoid

Close the switch and plot the magnetic field. The magnetic field is similar to the field around a bar magnet.

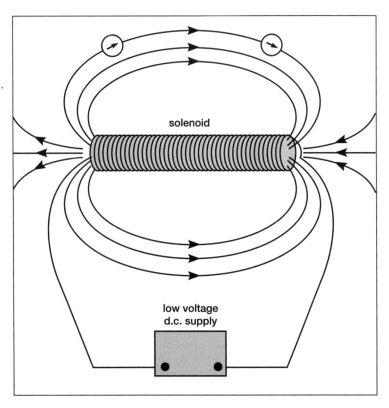

solenoid

low voltage d.c. supply

# CHEMISTRY

## CHAPTER 8. ELEMENTS, COMPOUNDS AND MIXTURES

## WHAT IS CHEMISTRY?

Chemistry is the study of substances and how they can be broken up and changed. Elements, compounds and mixtures, and all other substances are made up of particles.

**All matter is made up of particles.**

Movement of particles was first noticed by Robert Brown, who saw pollen grains zigzagging around in water. This movement is called **Brownian movement**.

Solids, liquids and gases are all made up of particles. Whether a substance is a solid, a liquid or a gas depends on how freely and how quickly the particles move.

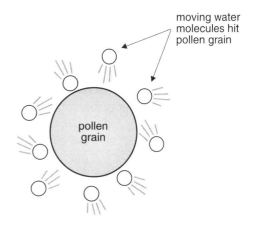

moving water molecules hit pollen grain

pollen grain

## ELEMENTS

### *Elements and atoms*

All substances are made up of tiny particles called atoms. When a substance is made up of only one type of atom it is called an element, e.g. the element iron is made up of iron atoms; the element hydrogen is made up of hydrogen atoms; the element sulphur is made up of sulphur atoms.

**An atom is the smallest particle of an element which still retains the properties of that element.**

**An element is a substance which cannot be broken down into simpler substances by chemical reactions.**

# COMPOUNDS

## Compounds and elements

When elements combine by means of a chemical reaction they form new substances called compounds. When the elements hydrogen and oxygen combine they form the compound water ($H_2O$).

**A compound is formed when two or more elements combine chemically.**

## Compounds and molecules

**A molecule is two or more atoms chemically combined**. It is the smallest particle of an element or a compound that can exist on its own.

Hydrogen, $H_2$, and oxygen, $O_2$, are compounds. They are made from molecules of elements.

Carbon dioxide, $CO_2$, and methane, $CH_4$, are compounds. They are made from molecules of compounds.

Sodium chloride, NaCl, and magnesium oxide, MgO, are compounds. The elements are joined together in giant structures called lattices and are not molecules.

# MIXTURES

## Mixtures and compounds

Not all substances are made up of elements combined chemically. Many are just mixed up or jumbled together. Substances like air, sea-water and crude oil are mixtures.

**A mixture is formed when two or more substances are put together but are not chemically combined.**

When sulphur and iron filings are mixed together they form a mixture.
When sulphur and iron filings are heated together they form a compound.

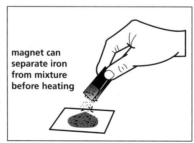

magnet can separate iron from mixture before heating

magnet cannot separate iron from substance after heating

## Differences between mixtures and compounds

| Mixture | Compound |
|---|---|
| Consists of two or more substances | Consists of a single substance |
| Amounts of the substances can vary | Amounts of the elements are fixed |
| Can often be separated easily | Can only be separated into its elements by a chemical reaction |
| Properties are similar to the substances used to make the mixture | Properties are very different to the elements used to make the compound |

## *Mixtures and solutions*

Solutions are a very common type of mixture. When a substance is mixed with a liquid the substance may dissolve in the liquid. The substance is said to be soluble in that liquid and the resulting mixture is called a solution.

- A **solvent** is the liquid in which the solution is made.
- A **solute** is the substance which dissolves in the solvent.
- A **solution** is a mixture of a solute and a solvent.

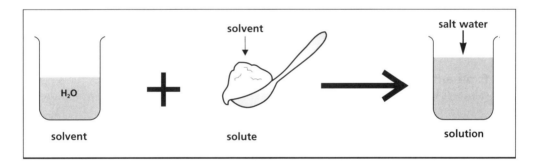

- A **dilute solution** contains a little solute in a lot of solvent.
- A **concentrated solution** contains a lot of solute in a little solvent.
- A **saturated solution** contains as much solute as can be dissolved at a given temperature.
- A **supersaturated solution** contains more solute than a saturated solution would at the same temperature.

## *Suspensions*

Suspensions are mixtures which often look like solutions. Salad cream, mayonnaise, emulsion paint, and muddy water are all familiar examples of suspensions. A suspension contains suspended solids spread throughout a liquid. Sometimes the suspended solids may fall to the bottom and form a sediment.

**A suspension is a mixture of a liquid and a finely divided insoluble solid.**

# PHYSICAL AND CHEMICAL CHANGES

### Physical changes

Ice changing into water, water changing into steam, and magnetising a piece of iron are examples of physical changes. In each case new properties may be gained but there is no change in mass.

**A physical change is a change in which no new substance is formed, but the original substance gains new properties.**

### Chemical changes

Burning of fuels, burning magnesium, and rusting of iron are examples of chemical changes.

**A chemical change is a change in which at least one new substance is formed.**

| Physical changes | Chemical changes |
|---|---|
| No new substances formed | One or more new substance formed |
| No change in mass | A change in mass |
| Can be easily reversed | Not easily reversed |
| Often no heat involved | Heat is usually involved |

**Exothermic reaction** is a reaction which gives out heat e.g. burning of fuels, neutralisation of an acid with a base. These reactions cause a rise in temperature.

**Endothermic reaction** is a reaction which requires heat e.g. dissolving ammonium nitrate or ammonium chloride in water. These reactions cause a fall in temperature.

**The law of conservation of matter: matter is neither created nor destroyed in a chemical reaction.**

The mass of the flash bulb after it flashes is the same as the mass before it flashes. This chemical reaction takes place in a sealed container, illustrating the law of conservation of matter.

Many substances are mixtures which may need to be separated. Crude oil is a mixture which is difficult to separate into gases such as methane, liquids such as petrol and tarry solids such as bitumen. Simple mixtures, such as sea-water, can be separated easily into water and salt.

Mixtures can be separated easily if the physical properties of the parts of each mixture are very different.

## SEPARATING SOLIDS FROM LIQUIDS

- **Decanting:** Large solids, such as potatoes, which do not dissolve in water can be removed by pouring the water off and leaving the solid behind.

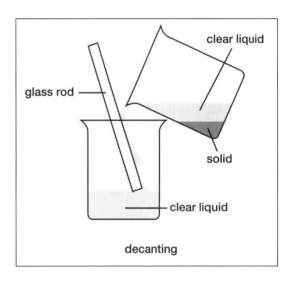

decanting

- **Filtration:** This is used to separate small insoluble solids from a liquid. The filter paper has tiny holes which let the liquid through, but are too small to allow the solid particles through. Sand can be separated from water by filtration.

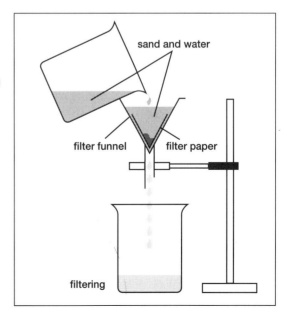

filtering

- **Evaporation:** This is used to separate a solid from its solution. Salt is obtained from a salt solution by heating the solution and allowing the water to evaporate, leaving the salt behind.

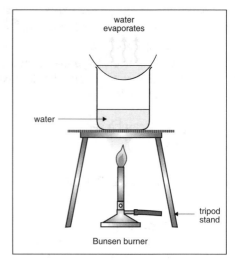

- **Crystallisation:** Solids can be separated from a concentrated solution by being allowed to crystallise.

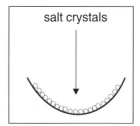

## SEPARATING LIQUIDS FROM LIQUIDS

- **Distillation:** Solids can be separated from a solution. Distillation is usually used to separate liquids.

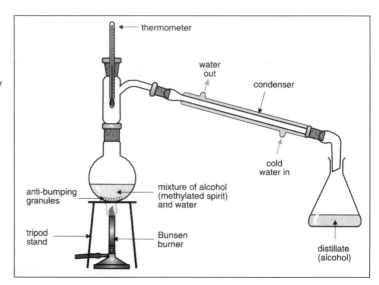

- **Decanting:** This is used to separate two liquids which do not mix, such as oil and water.

- **Using a separating funnel:**
  Immiscible liquids are liquids which do not mix. Oil is separated from water by allowing the denser liquid (water) to run off into the beaker. The tap is closed and the oil is left behind in the separating funnel.

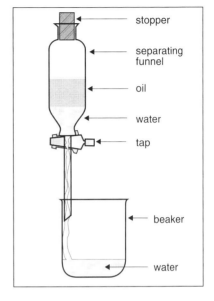

- **Distillation:** This is **evaporation followed by condensation**. It is used to separate miscible liquids with different boiling points.

## SEPARATING A SOLID FROM A SOLID BY SUBLIMATION

In sublimation a substance changes from a solid directly into a gas when heated.

A solid can be separated from another solid by sublimation if one of the solids can sublime. Ammonium chloride can be separated from sodium chloride in this way.

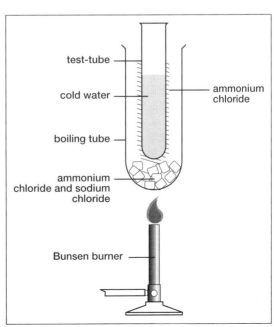

## CHROMATOGRAPHY

Chromatography is used to separate small amounts of substances in a mixture. A small sample of colouring can be separated into different colours by paper chromatography.

Paper chromatography is a method of separating substances by allowing a solvent to carry them different distances along a filter paper.

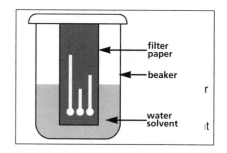

filter paper

beaker

r

water solvent

it

---

## CHAPTER 10. AIR AND FUELS

# AIR

Air contains a mixture of gases: 78 % nitrogen, $N_2$, 21 % oxygen, $O_2$, 1% argon, Ar, and 0.04 % carbon dioxide, $CO_2$. The amount of water vapour in the air varies from day to day and from place to place. The air around us is a vital resource: oxygen is necessary for breathing, while carbon dioxide is necessary for photosynthesis.

**Air contains approximately 21 % oxygen.**

1. The original volume of air = 100 $cm^3$.
2. Air is pushed backwards and forwards over the heated copper.
3. The volume of air after heating  = 79 %.
4. The percentage of oxygen in air  = 21 %.

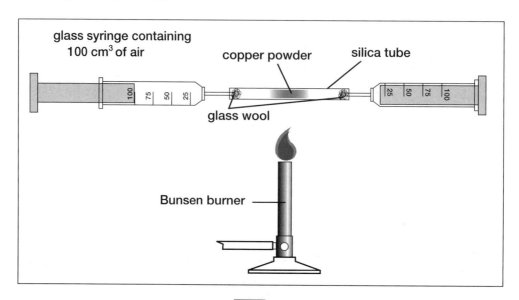

glass syringe containing 100 $cm^3$ of air

copper powder

silica tube

glass wool

Bunsen burner

**Air contains carbon dioxide and water vapour**.

As air is drawn through, the limewater turns milky.

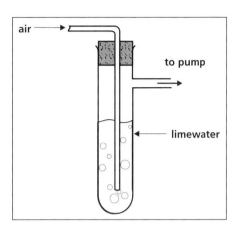

**Air contains water vapour**

Drops of liquid condense on the cold surface. When the liquid is added to anhydrous copper sulphate it changes the copper sulphate powder blue, showing that the liquid is water.

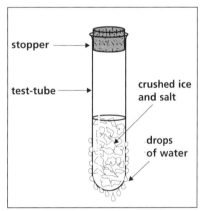

*Oxygen - the reactive gas*

**Preparation of oxygen**

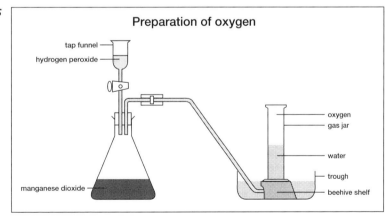

Preparation of oxygen

1. Add hydrogen peroxide solution slowly to the manganese dioxide.
2. Hydrogen peroxide + manganese dioxide (catalyst) ⇒ oxygen + water.
   $2H_2O_2$ + $MnO_2$ ⇒ $O_2$ + $2H_2O$
3. In the test for oxygen, a glowing splint relights.

**A catalyst is a substance which changes the speed of a chemical reaction.**

## Burning metals and non-metals in oxygen

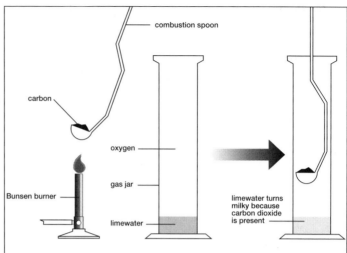

1. Heat the element in the oxygen.
2. Plunge the burning element into a gas jar of oxygen.
3. Add some water to the gas jar and shake.
4. Test to see whether the solution is acidic or basic.
5. Carbon + oxygen ⇒ carbon dioxide (acidic oxide).
6. Magnesium + oxygen ⇒ magnesium oxide (basic oxide).

## Properties and uses of oxygen

| Physical properties | Chemical properties | Uses |
|---|---|---|
| Colourless, odourless, tasteless gas | Does not burn, but supports combustion | Breathing |
| Slightly soluble in water | No effect on litmus | Welding and cutting |
| Slightly heavier than air | Reacts with metals and with non-metals to form oxides | Steel making |

*Carbon dioxide*

**Preparation of carbon dioxide**

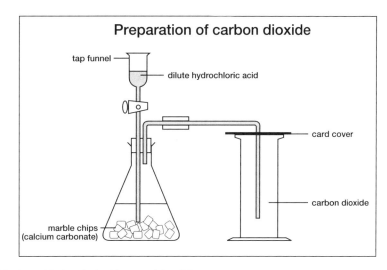

## Preparation of carbon dioxide

tap funnel

dilute hydrochloric acid

card cover

carbon dioxide

marble chips (calcium carbonate)

1. Add dilute hydrochloric acid slowly to the marble chips.
2. Calcium carbonate + hydrochloric acid $\Rightarrow$ calcium chloride + water + carbon dioxide.
   $CaCO_3$ + $2HCl$ $\Rightarrow$ $CaCl_2$ + $H_2O$ + $CO_2$
3. In the test for carbon dioxide, the limewater turns milky.

**Properties and uses of carbon dioxide**

| Physical properties | Chemical properties | Uses |
|---|---|---|
| Colourless, odourless, tasteless gas | Does not support combustion | Fire extinguishers |
| Slightly soluble in water | Acidic - turns blue litmus red | Fizzy drinks |
| Heavier than air | Turns limewater milky | Fridges |

## FIRE AND FUELS

- **Fuel:** any substance used to produce heat from a chemical or nuclear reaction.
- **Burning;** a rapid chemical reaction in which a fuel reacts with oxygen to produce heat.
- **Fossil fuels:** formed from the remains of plants and animals.
- **Fire:** three conditions are necessary to light a fire - fuel, heat and oxygen.

- **Fire extinguishers:** water, carbon dioxide, foam, dry powder and halon.

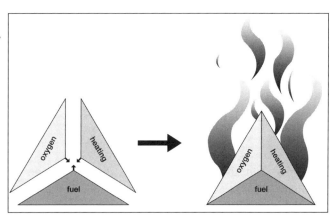

Water is the most common liquid on earth. All living things need water to survive. We use water every day of our lives - to drink, to wash, and to get rid of waste. Water is more important than food: we can survive for weeks without food, but only for a few days without water.

- **Water is a compound**. It is a molecule made up of one oxygen atom joined to two hydrogen atoms.

- **Water exists as a solid, as a liquid and as a gas on earth**. It melts at 0 $^{\circ}$C and boils at 100 $^{\circ}$C.

- **Water expands as it freezes**. This means that ice is less dense than water. Ice floats on water and acts as an insulator, preventing the water below from freezing.

- **Water is an excellent solvent.** Almost everything dissolves in water to some extent.

- **Water has high surface tension.** It seems to have a skin on its surface. This allows a needle to float on water and insects to walk on water.

- **Surface tension.** This is the force between the molecules at the surface of the water which holds the surface molecules tightly together like a skin.

- **Water rises up narrow tubes.** This is called capillarity. It allows water to rise up through plants.

- **Tests for water.** Water turns anhydrous copper sulphate blue; it turns cobalt chloride paper from blue to pink.

## THE WATER CYCLE

Water supplies are renewed constantly by a cycle of evaporation from the earth and rain from the clouds in the atmosphere.

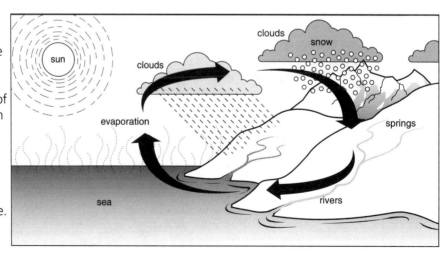

Heat from the sun causes evaporation from rivers, lakes and seas. The vapour condenses and forms clouds. These clouds then cool and form large droplets which can fall as rain, hail, sleet or snow.

## WATER TREATMENT

It is possible to drink rain-water. Water flowing over land may pick up all sorts of solids and liquids, and bacteria and parasites which may cause sickness or give a nasty taste or smell. Water is purified at a water works, making it safe to drink.

- **Screening**: Water is passed through a mesh to remove floating debris, such as plastic bags and wood.

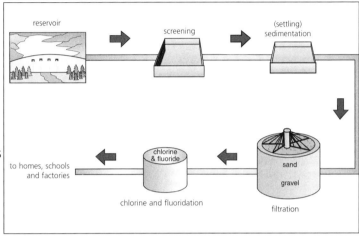

- **Settling:** Aluminium sulphate is added to the water. This allows the tiny suspended solids to stick together and form large clumps which settle on the bottom of the settling tank.
- **Filtration:** Water is filtered through filter beds consisting of gravel and fine sand.
- **Chlorination:** Chlorine is added to water to kill any bacteria.
- **Fluoridation:** Some countries, such as Ireland, are obliged by law to add fluoride to water to help prevent tooth decay.

## WATER HARDNESS

**Soft water** forms a lather easily with soap.

**Hard water** does not form a lather easily with soap. It forms a scum.

**Temporary hardness** can be removed by boiling. It is caused by calcium hydrogencarbonate dissolved in the water. Heating converts the soluble calcium hydrogencarbonate into insoluble calcium carbonate.

calcium hydrogencarbonate $\overset{heat}{\Rightarrow}$ calcium carbonate + carbon dioxide + water

$Ca(HCO_3)_2$ $\overset{heat}{\Rightarrow}$ $CaCO_3$ + $CO_2$ + $H_2O$

**Permanent hardness** cannot be removed by boiling. It is caused by the presence of calcium sulphate, calcium chloride, magnesium sulphate or magnesium chloride dissolved in the water. Permanent hardness is removed by distillation, by adding washing soda or by ion exchange.

| Hardness | Cause | Removal |
|---|---|---|
| Temporary | Calcium hydrogencarbonate | Boiling<br>Distillation<br>Ion exchange |
| Permanent | Calcium chloride<br>Calcium sulphate<br>Magnesium sulphate<br>Magnesium chloride | Distillation<br>Washing soda (bath salts)<br>Ion exchange |

## Advantages and disadvantages of hard water

| Advantages | Disadvantages |
|---|---|
| Nicer taste | Blocks pipes by producing limescale |
| Good for brewing and tanning | Wastes soap |
| Provides calcium for bones and teeth | Produces scum |

## Investigating hardness in water

Three different water samples, distilled water, water with temporary hardness and water with permanent hardness, are tested with a soap solution (or soap flakes) to see how easily they form a lather.

1. Place 20 cm³ of each water sample into three conical flasks.
2. Measure the amount of soap solution necessary to form a lather. This will identify the distilled water.
3. Boil samples of the two types of hard water in a water bath. This removes temporary hardness from the water.
4. Measure the amount of soap solution necessary to form a lather.
5. The water with permanent hardness does not form a lather easily.

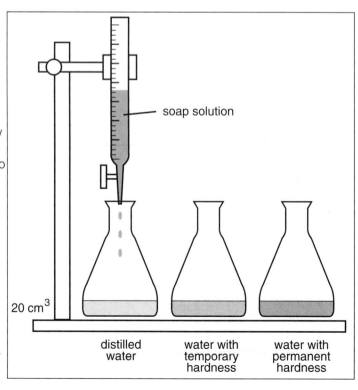

soap solution

20 cm³

distilled water | water with temporary hardness | water with permanent hardness

# ATOMS

Atoms are made up of small particles called sub-atomic particles. These are protons, neutrons and electrons. The mass of a proton and a neutron are the same, 1 atomic mass unit (amu). The mass of an electron is so small compared to a proton (1/1840) or neutron that we do not count its mass.

| Particle | Mass | Charge | Location |
|----------|------|--------|----------|
| Proton | 1 | Positive | Nucleus |
| Electron | 0 | Negative | Electron cloud |
| Neutron | 1 | Neutral | Nucleus |

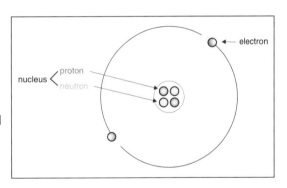

### Arrangement of electrons in atoms

Electrons move around the nucleus in orbits. Each orbit can hold a certain number of electrons. The first orbit is full when it contains two electrons, the next orbit is full when it contains eight electrons, and the next orbit is also full when it contains eight electrons.

### Atoms with full orbits (shells)

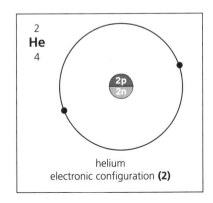

helium
electronic configuration **(2)**

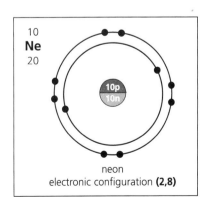

neon
electronic configuration **(2,8)**

## Some other atoms

Atomic number  ←  **1**  →  Number of protons  (+)  = 1
Number of electrons (-)  = 1

**H**

Mass number  ←  **1**  →  Number of neutrons = 1 - 1 = 0

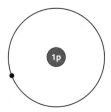

Hydrogen
electronic configuration **(1)**

Atomic number  ←  **3**  →  Number of protons  (+)  = 3
Number of electrons (-)  = 3

**Li**

Mass number  ←  **7**  →  Number of neutrons = 7 - 3 = 4

Lithium
electronic configuration **(2,1)**

Atomic number  ←  **11**  →  Number of protons  (+)  = 11
Number of electrons (-)  = 11

**Na**

Mass number  ←  **23**  →  Number of neutrons = 23-11 =12

Sodium
electronic configuration **(2,8,1)**

Atomic number  ←  **17**  →  Number of protons  (+)  = 17
Number of electrons (-)  = 17

**Cl**

Mass number  ←  **35**  →  Number of neutrons = 35-17
  = 18

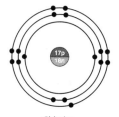

Chlorine
electronic configuration **(2,8,7)**

# BONDS

## Chemical bonds

Atoms combine with each other to form compounds. When they join with each other atoms try to have full outer shells (either 2 or 8 electrons).

Atoms combine with each other by forming chemical bonds. A chemical bond is the 'glue' that holds a compound together.

Ionic bonds and covalent bonds are the main types of chemical bond.

## Ionic bonding

An ion is an electrically-charged atom or group of atoms. An ionic bond is formed when electrons are transferred between atoms.

Positive ions are formed by the loss of electrons. Negative ions are formed by the gain of electrons.

**An ionic bond is formed by the attractive force between a positive and a negative ion.**

Sodium chloride (NaCl)

Sodium has one electron in its outer shell which it wants to lose in order to have a full outer orbit. Chlorine has seven electrons in its outer shell: it needs to gain one electron in order to have a full outer shell.

Sodium reacts with chlorine by transferring the electron in its outer shell to chlorine. The sodium atom becomes a positive ion and the chlorine atom becomes a negative ion. These oppositely-charged ions attract each other and form the compound sodium chloride.

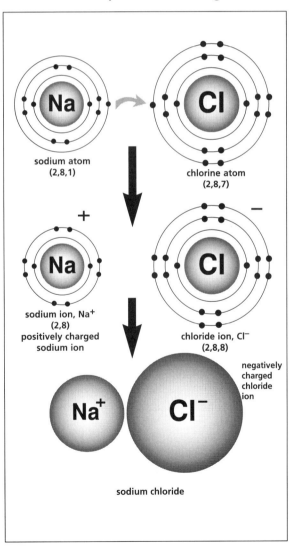

sodium atom
(2,8,1)

chlorine atom
(2,8,7)

+

sodium ion, Na⁺
(2,8)
positively charged
sodium ion

−

chloride ion, Cl⁻
(2,8,8)

negatively charged chloride ion

Na⁺   Cl⁻

sodium chloride

## Ionic crystals

Ionic crystals are made up of millions of ions joined together in a regular arrangement called a lattice. Each sodium ion is surrounded by chloride ions and each chloride ion is surrounded by sodium ions.

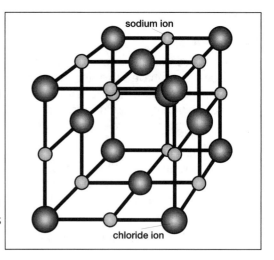

## *Covalent bonding*

Not all atoms want to transfer electrons from one to the other. Some non-metals share electrons with each other. In this way they can obtain full outer shells (2 electrons or 8 electrons).

**A covalent bond is formed by the sharing of electrons between atoms.**

## The hydrogen molecule ($H_2$)

A hydrogen atom has one electron in its outer shell. Hydrogen needs two electrons to have a full outer shell.

When two hydrogen atoms come close enough to each other, their outer shells overlap and they share a pair of electrons. Each hydrogen atom is in a stable state because each has two electrons in its outer shell. This sharing of electrons is called a covalent bond.

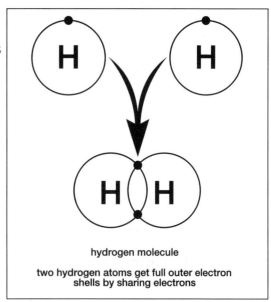

hydrogen molecule

two hydrogen atoms get full outer electron shells by sharing electrons

## The chlorine molecule ($Cl_2$)

A chlorine atom has seven electrons in its outer shell. Chlorine needs eight electrons to have a full outer shell.

When two chlorine atoms come close enough to each other, their outer shells overlap and they share a pair of electrons. Each chlorine atom is in a stable state because each has eight electrons in its outer shell. This sharing of electrons is called a covalent bond.

The water molecule ($H_2O$)

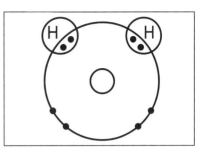

An oxygen atom has six electrons in its outer shell.
Oxygen needs eight electrons to have a full outer shell.

When an oxygen atom comes close enough to two
hydrogen atoms, their outer shells overlap and oxygen
shares a pair of electrons with each hydrogen atom.
The oxygen atom is in a stable state because it has
eight electrons in its outer shell, while at the same
time the hydrogen atoms are in a stable state because they have two electrons in their
outer shells.

## Properties of ionic and covalent compounds

| Ionic | Covalent |
|---|---|
| Usually crystalline solids | Usually liquids or gases |
| High melting points and boiling points | Low melting points and boiling points |
| Consist of giant lattices | Consist of separate molecules |
| Usually soluble in water | Usually insoluble in water |
| Conduct electricity when melted or in solution | Do not conduct electricity |

## CHAPTER 13. GROUPS OF ELEMENTS AND THE PERIODIC TABLE

# GROUPS OF ELEMENTS

In a supermarket similar items are arranged into groups, e.g. apples are on one shelf,
oranges are on another, and breakfast cereals are on another shelf.

Elements, like the items on the supermarket shelves, can be arranged into groups.
Elements with similar physical and chemical properties are arranged into groups.

## THE PERIODIC TABLE

**The periodic table is an arrangement of elements in order of increasing atomic
mass**.

Mendeleev arranged the periodic table in this way and also put elements with similar
properties in the same vertical column (see the Periodic Table at the beginning of this
book).

**Vertical columns** of similar elements are called **groups,** e.g. Group 1 contains the similar
elements, lithium, sodium and potassium.

The properties of the elements in any group gradually change as you move down a group.

The **horizontal rows** are called **periods.** The elements on the left-hand side and in the middle of the periodic table are metals, while the elements on the far right-hand side are non-metals.

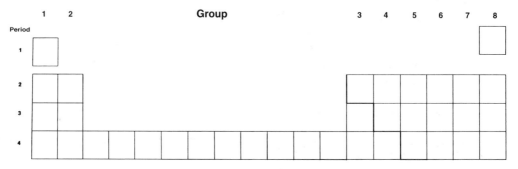

## Group 1: The alkali metals

Lithium, sodium, potassium, rubidium and caesium are called the alkali metals because they react with water to form alkaline solutions. They have similar physical and chemical properties because they each have one electron in their outer shell. They are soft, shiny metals which are stored in oil because they react with air and water.

Reactions

- with water:

sodium + water $\Rightarrow$ sodium hydroxide + hydrogen

$2 \, Na \quad + \quad 2 \, H_2O \quad \Rightarrow \quad 2 \, NaOH \quad + \quad H_2$

- with oxygen:

lithium + oxygen $\Rightarrow$ lithium oxide

$4 \, Li \quad + \quad O_2 \quad \Rightarrow \quad 2 \, Li_2O$

- with dilute acid:

sodium + hydrochloric acid $\Rightarrow$ sodium chloride + hydrogen

$2 \, Na \quad + \quad 2 \, HCl \quad \Rightarrow \quad 2 \, NaCl \quad + \quad H_2$

| Name | Symbol | Electronic configuration | Reaction with water |
|------|--------|--------------------------|---------------------|
| Lithium | Li | 2 1 | Gentle |
| Sodium | Na | 2 8 1 | Vigorous |
| Potassium | K | 2 8 8 1 | Violent and dangerous |

## Group 2: Alkaline earth metals

The best known alkaline earth metals are magnesium and calcium. They have similar physical and chemical properties because they each have two electrons in their outer shell.

Reactions

- with water:

  magnesium   + water   $\Rightarrow$   magnesium oxide   + hydrogen

  Mg   + $H_2O$   $\Rightarrow$   MgO   +   $H_2$

- with oxygen:

  calcium   + oxygen   $\Rightarrow$   calcium oxide

  2 Ca   + $O_2$   $\Rightarrow$   2 CaO

- with dilute acid:

  magnesium   + hydrochloric acid   $\Rightarrow$   magnesium chloride   + hydrogen

  Mg   + 2 HCl   $\Rightarrow$   $MgCl_2$   +   $H_2$

| Name | Symbol | Electronic configuration | Reaction with water |
|------|--------|--------------------------|---------------------|
| Magnesium | Mg | 2 8 2 | Reacts when heated |
| Calcium | Na | 2 8 8 2 | Vigorous |

## Group 7: The halogens

The best known halogens are fluorine, chlorine, bromine and iodine. They have similar physical and chemical properties because they each have seven electrons in their outer shell.

Fluorine and chlorine are gases, bromine is a liquid and iodine is a solid.

| Name | Symbol | Electronic configuration | State |
|------|--------|--------------------------|-------|
| Fluorine | F | 2 7 | Gas |
| Chlorine | Cl | 2 8 7 | Gas |
| Bromine | Br | 2 8 8 7 | Liquid |
| Iodine | I | 2 8 8 18 7 | Solid |

# CHEMICAL FORMULAS OF COMPOUNDS

*Valency: combining power*

The chemical formula of a compound is worked out by finding out the combining power of the atoms. Atoms combine with other atoms when they have the same combining power. One sodium atom combines with one chlorine atom because each has the same combining power: sodium wants to lose **one** electron, while chlorine wants to gain **one** electron. Sodium and chlorine have the same combining power: this is called valency.

**The valency of an atom is the number of electrons lost, gained or shared by that atom in a chemical bond.**

In general, the valency of an atom is found from the group number on the periodic table.

| Group | 1 | 2 | 3 | 4 | 5 | 6 | 7 |
|---------|---|---|---|---|---|---|---|
| Valency | 1 | 2 | 3 | 4 | 3 | 2 | 1 |

**The valency of an ion is the same as the electrical charge on the ion**.

| Name of ion | Formula | Valency |
|---|---|---|
| Hydroxide | $OH^-$ | 1 |
| Nitrate | $NO_3^-$ | 1 |
| Sulphate | $SO_4^{2-}$ | 2 |
| Carbonate | $CO_3^{2-}$ | 2 |
| Hydrogencarbonate | $HCO_3^{2-}$ | 1 |
| Ammonium | $NH_4^+$ | 1 |

**Examples:**

Na + Cl $\Rightarrow$ (Na)(Cl) sodium chloride, NaCl
Group 1    7
Valency 1    1

Li + F $\Rightarrow$ (Li)(F) lithium fluoride, LiF
Group 1    7
Valency 1    1

|         | Mg | + | O  | ⇒ |
|---------|----|---|----|---|
| Group   | 2  |   | 6  |   |
| Valency | 2  |   | 2  |   |

magnesium oxide, MgO

|         | Mg | + | Cl | ⇒ |
|---------|----|---|----|---|
| Group   | 2  |   | 7  |   |
| Valency | 2  |   | 1  |   |

magnesium chloride, $MgCl_2$

|         | Na | + | OH | ⇒ |
|---------|----|---|----|---|
| Valency | 1  |   | 1  |   |

sodium hydroxide, NaOH

|         | K  | + | OH | ⇒ |
|---------|----|---|----|---|
| Valency | 1  |   | 1  |   |

potassium hydroxide, KOH

|         | Na | + | $NO_3$ | ⇒ |
|---------|----|---|--------|---|
| Valency | 1  |   | 1      |   |

sodium nitrate, $NaNO_3$

|         | Mg | + | $NO_3$ | ⇒ |
|---------|----|---|--------|---|
| Valency | 2  |   | 1      |   |

magnesium nitrate, $Mg(NO_3)_2$

|         | Na | + | $SO_4$ | ⇒ |
|---------|----|---|--------|---|
| Valency | 1  |   | 1      |   |

sodium sulphate, $Na_2SO_4$

## BALANCING CHEMICAL EQUATIONS

During a chemical reaction, substances react with each other. The substances which react with each other are called the reactants. The new substances formed during the reaction are called the products.

**reactants ⇒ products**

### Rules for balancing equations

Example: Magnesium reacts with oxygen to form magnesium oxide.

1. Make sure you know what the reactants and the products are.
2. Write a word equation for the reaction.
   magnesium + oxygen ⇒ magnesium oxide
3. Write in the correct formula for each element or compound.
   $Mg + O_2 ⇒ MgO$
4. Balance the number of each type of atoms on either side.

There are 2 oxygen atoms (O atoms) on the left but only 1 oxygen atom on the right. To balance the number of O atoms we need to double the number of O atoms on the right. This is done by doubling the amount of MgO.

$$Mg + O_2 ⇒ \textbf{2}\,MgO$$

Now there are 2 magnesium atoms on the right but only 1 magnesium atom on the left. So we need to double the amount of magnesium on the left.

$$\textbf{2}\,Mg + O_2 ⇒ \textbf{2}\,MgO$$

Example: Sodium reacts with water to form sodium hydroxide and hydrogen.
1. Make sure you know what the reactants and the products are.
2. Write a word equation for the reaction.
   sodium + water ⇒ sodium hydroxide + hydrogen
3. Write in the correct formula for each element or compound.
   $Na + H_2O ⇒ NaOH + H_2$
4. Balance the number of each type of atoms on either side.

There are 2 hydrogen atoms (H atoms) on the left and a total of (1 + 2) hydrogen atoms on the right. If we double the number of H atoms on the left we have then a total of 4 H atoms on the left.

$$Na + \textbf{2}\,H_2O ⇒ NaOH + H_2$$

We balance the H atoms by doubling the amount of NaOH on the right. This means we have 4 H atoms on each side ( 2 x 2 = 1 x 2 + 2).

$$Na \ + \ 2\,H_2O \ \Rightarrow \ 2\,NaOH \ + \ H_2$$

Now there are 2 sodium atoms on the right, but only 1 sodium atom on the left. So we need to double the amount of sodium on the left.

$$2\,Na \ + \ 2\,H_2O \ \Rightarrow \ 2\,NaOH \ + \ H_2$$

## CHAPTER 15. ACIDS AND BASES

# ACIDS

Acids are usually recognised by simple properties such as taste, how they react with indicators and how they react with each other. Some acids, such as hydrochloric acid, nitric acid and sulphuric acid, are very dangerous. These acids attack metals, stone, clothing and flesh. Other acids, such as carbonic acid in soft drinks, lactic acid in milk and citric acid in fruit, are not dangerous.

### Properties of acids

- Acids have a sour taste. Vinegar and citric acids have a stinging sour taste.
- Acids are corrosive. They attack metals, stone, materials and flesh.
- **Acids turn blue litmus red**.
- Acids have a **pH less than 7.** Strong acids, such as hydrochloric acid, have a pH close to 0, while weak acids, such as milk, are close to 7.
- Most acids react with most metals to form salts and to release hydrogen gas.
     metal    +    acid    ⇒    salt    +    hydrogen
- Acids react with carbonates to give carbon dioxide gas.
     carbonate  +   acid     ⇒    salt   +  carbon dioxide  +  water
- Acids neutralise bases by forming a salt and water. This is called neutralisation.
     acid       +    base   ⇒    salt    +    water

## BASES

Bases are the opposite to acids. Bases that are soluble in water are called alkalis. Alkalis are soapy to touch because they react with the natural oils on the skin to make soap.

- Bases are corrosive.
- **Bases turn red litmus blue**.
- Bases have a **pH greater than 7.** Ammonia has a pH close to 7, while sodium hydroxide has a pH nearer to 14.
- Ammonia, metal hydroxides and metal oxides are bases.
- Bases neutralise acids by forming a salt and water.

## Neutralisation

When an acid is mixed with a base they react and cancel each other out by forming a salt and water. This is called neutralisation.

## Indicators and pH

The easiest way to see whether a substance is an acid or a base is to see what colour it changes an indicator like litmus. Litmus is red in acid and blue in base. Red cabbage indicator and methyl orange are other common indicators.

**Indicators are substances which change colour depending on whether they are in an acidic or an alkaline solution.**

## The pH scale

An indicator can tell us only whether a substance is an acid or a base. If we want to know the measure of the acidity or basicity we use a scale called the pH scale. The scale goes from 0 to 14.

On the pH scale :
*   acids are less than 7.
*   neutral solutions, such as water, are equal to 7.
*   bases are greater than 7.

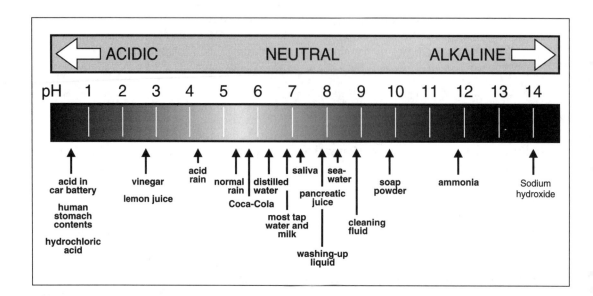

## Finding the pH of different substances

1. Place samples of a number of substances in test-tubes.
2. Add a drop of universal indicator to each sample.
3. Compare the colour obtained with the colour on the colour chart.

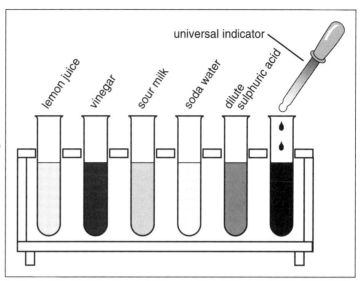

## *Reactions of acids*

- **metal  +  acid  $\Rightarrow$  salt  +  hydrogen**

  Zinc reacts with dilute hydrochloric acid to form zinc chloride and to release hydrogen gas.

  $Zn  +  2 HCl \Rightarrow ZnCl_2  + H_2$

- **carbonate + acid  $\Rightarrow$  salt + carbon dioxide + water**

  Acids react with carbonates to form a salt and to release carbon dioxide gas and form water.

  $CaCO_3  + 2 HCl \Rightarrow CaCl_2  +  CO_2  + H_2O$

- **acid  +  base  $\Rightarrow$  salt  +  water**

  Acids neutralise bases by forming a salt and water.

  $HCl  +  NaOH \Rightarrow NaCl  +  H_2O$

## Preparation of a salt

1. Add sodium hydroxide solution to the conical flask using a pipette.

2. Add hydrochloric acid solution from the burette to the sodium hydroxide solution until the indicator changes colour.

3. Repeat the procedure without the indicator.

4. Evaporate the water from the salt solution to obtain a dry sample of sodium chloride.

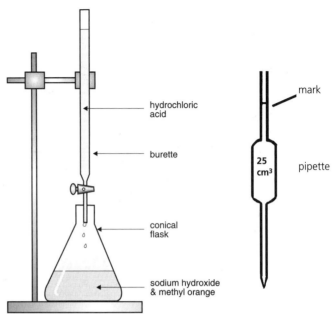

### Some common acids and bases

| Acid | Formula | Base | Formula |
|------|---------|------|---------|
| Hydrochloric acid | HCl | Sodium hydroxide | NaOH |
| Nitric acid | $HNO_3$ | Potassium hydroxide | KOH |
| Sulphuric acid | $H_2SO_4$ | Sodium hydrogencarbonate | $NaHCO_3$ |
| Carbonic acid | $H_2CO_3$ | Magnesium oxide | MgO |
| Ethanoic acid | $CH_3COOH$ | Ammonia | $NH_3$ |

### Acid rain

Normal rain-water is slightly acidic. Carbon dioxide in the air reacts with the rain-water to form a weak acid called carbonic acid. This has a pH of about 5.5.

$$\text{carbon dioxide} \quad + \quad \text{water} \quad \Rightarrow \quad \text{carbonic acid}$$
$$CO_2 \quad + \quad H_2O \quad \Rightarrow \quad H_2CO_3$$

Power stations, factories, motor vehicles and homes burn fuels which give off fumes into the atmosphere. These fumes contain sulphur dioxide ($SO_2$) and oxides of nitrogen ($NO_x$).

These oxides react with rain-water and form sulphuric acid and nitric acid. These strong acids lower the pH below the normal value of 5.5.

Acid rain kills trees, damages crops, releases harmful metals into soil, destroys buildings and harms aquatic species.

**Acid rain is rain-water with a pH of less than that of normal rain-water (5.5).**

# METALS

## *Some properties of metals*

Metals:
- are lustrous and shiny.
- are malleable - they can be hammered and shaped.
- are ductile - they can be stretched.
- are usually strong hard solids. Sodium and the other alkali metals are soft. A few metals, such as mercury, are liquids.
- are good conductors of heat and electricity. Heat energy and electrons can move easily through metals.
- have high melting points. Iron melts at 1540 $^\circ$C.

## Alloys
**Alloys are mixtures of metals, e.g. steel is a mixture of iron, carbon and other metals, and is much harder than pure iron.**

## Conduction of heat

The wax melts first on the metals because metals are good conductors.

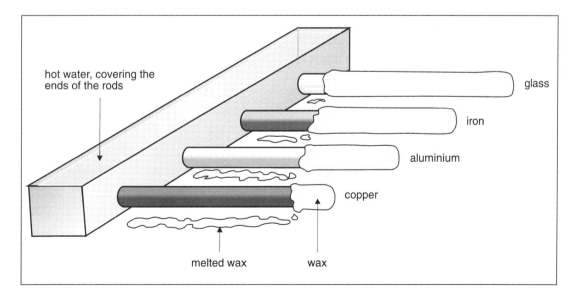

## Conduction of electricity

When a metal is tested, the bulb lights because metals are good conductors.

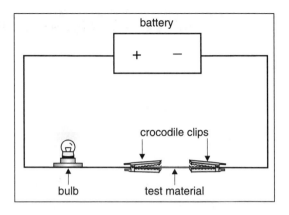

## Corrosion

When metals react with oxygen they corrode. This causes an increase in mass.

This is an oxidation reaction. Iron and copper corrode quite easily, while zinc and nickel do not corrode easily.

Corrosion returns metals to their ore, e.g. iron is changed into iron oxide.

Rusting is iron corrosion. Water and oxygen are necessary for rusting.

Corrosion can be prevented by painting, electroplating, greasing, galvanising, anodising and alloying.

## Conditions necessary for rusting

1. Leave the test-tubes to stand for a few days.
2. Rusting takes place in A and in C. Both contain oxygen and water.
3. C has the greatest amount of rust because it contains more oxygen than A.

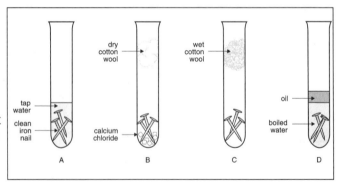

## Reactivity of metals

**The activity series**

← ——————————————————— *Most reactive*

potassium, sodium, calcium, magnesium, zinc, iron, copper, silver, gold

Reactive metals such as sodium are never found free in nature, while unreactive metals such as silver and gold are found free in nature.

## Reaction when heated in air or with oxygen

Almost all metals react with oxygen to form basic oxides (turn red litmus blue). Some metals, such as silver and gold, do not react with oxygen.

$$
\text{magnesium} \quad + \quad \text{oxygen} \quad \overset{\text{heat}}{\Rightarrow} \quad \text{magnesium oxide}
$$

$$
2\ Mg \quad + \quad O_2 \quad \overset{\text{heat}}{\Rightarrow} \quad 2\ MgO
$$

$$
\text{silver} \quad + \quad \text{oxygen} \quad \Rightarrow \quad \text{no reaction}
$$

## Reaction with water

Metals such as potassium and sodium react violently with cold water. Calcium reacts vigorously with cold water, while magnesium reacts vigorously with hot water. Copper, silver and gold do not react with water.

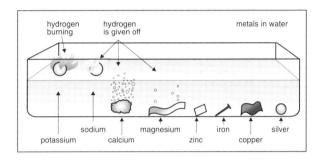

$$
\text{sodium} \quad + \quad \text{water} \quad \Rightarrow \quad \text{sodium hydroxide} \quad + \quad \text{hydrogen}
$$
$$
2\ Na \quad + \quad 2\ H_2O \quad \Rightarrow \quad 2\ NaOH \quad + \quad H_2
$$

$$
\text{magnesium} \quad + \quad \text{steam} \quad \Rightarrow \quad \text{magnesium oxide} \quad + \quad \text{hydrogen}
$$
$$
Mg \quad + \quad H_2O \quad \Rightarrow \quad MgO \quad + \quad H_2
$$

$$
\text{silver} \quad + \quad \text{water} \quad \Rightarrow \quad \text{no reaction}
$$

## Reaction with dilute acids

**When metals react with dilute hydrochloric acid they form salts and release hydrogen gas.**

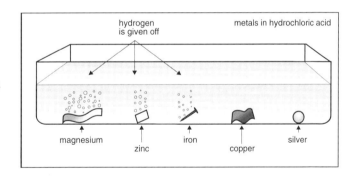

Metals like potassium and sodium react explosively with cold water. Calcium reacts violently with cold water, while magnesium reacts vigorously with hot water. Silver and gold do not react with water.

$$
\text{magnesium} \quad + \quad \text{dilute hydrochloric acid} \quad \Rightarrow \quad \text{magnesium oxide} \quad + \quad \text{hydrogen}
$$

$$
Mg \quad + \quad HCl \quad \Rightarrow \quad MgCl_2 \quad + \quad H_2
$$

$$
\text{gold} \quad + \quad \text{dilute acid} \quad \Rightarrow \quad \text{no reaction}
$$

## Summary of the reactions of metals

| Metal | Heating with oxygen | Reaction with water | Reaction with dilute hydrochloric acid |
|---|---|---|---|
| Potassium Sodium | Form oxide easily | Vigorous reaction, burn with coloured flame Float and form metal hydroxide and release hydrogen gas | Dangerous and explosive reactions Produce salt and release hydrogen gas |
| Calcium | Forms oxides slowly | Forms metal hydroxide and releases hydrogen gas | Produces salt and releases hydrogen gas |
| Magnesium Zinc Iron | Form oxides slowly No reaction | Form metal hydroxide and release hydrogen gas | |
| Copper Silver Gold | No reaction | No reaction | No reaction |

Potassium, sodium and calcium should be handled carefully using a tongs.

### *Metals and electricity*

Simple cell

**A simple cell is made from two metals and an electrolyte.**

**An electrolyte is a solution that conducts an electric current.**

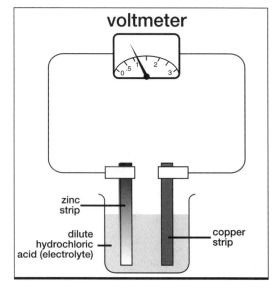

## Different combinations of metals produce different voltages

Reactive metals high up in the activity series lose electrons easily. The further the metals are apart in the activity series, the greater is the voltage produced.

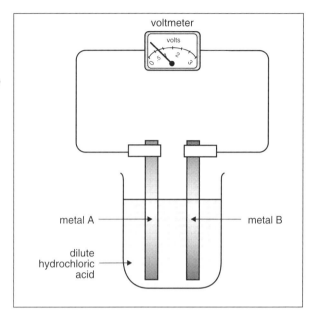

The dry cell

- **Positive electrode -** carbon and manganese dioxide
- **Negative electrode -** zinc
- **Electrolyte -** ammonium chloride

The advantages of a dry cell over a simple cell are that the dry cell produces a steady 1.5 volts, contains no liquid, and is compact and portable.

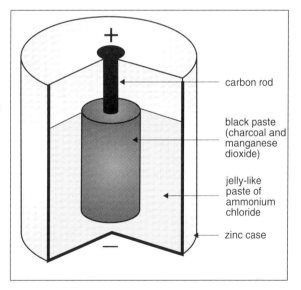

## Electrolysis

Hydrogen gas collects at the negative electrode. When lighted it 'pops'.

Oxygen gas collects at the positive electrode. It relights a glowing splint.

Water is a compound of hydrogen and oxygen. Twice as much hydrogen as oxygen is produced.

**Electrolysis is the chemical breakdown of an electrolyte when an electric current is passed through it.**

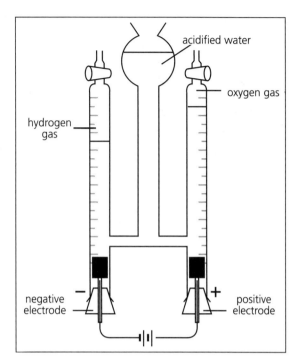

## Electroplating

One metal may be coated on to another by electrolysis.

If you allow a small current to flow for about 15 - 20 minutes, a layer of copper will stick on to the steel.

Electroplating:

- improves appearance of cheaper metals, such as gold-plated jewellery.
- prevents corrosion. EPNS cutlery is electroplated nickel silver.

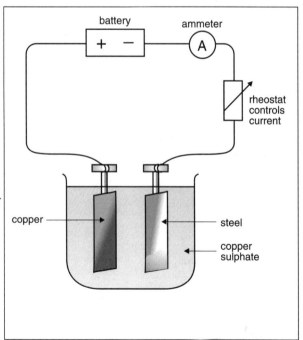

# BIOLOGY

## CHAPTER 17. LIVING THINGS

**Biology is the study of living things**.

All living things (organisms) have certain common characteristics**.**

### Characteristics of living things
- **Feeding:** All living things need food for energy. Plants make their own food; animals eat plants and other animals.
- **Respiration:** All animals and plants release energy from food.
- **Movement and sensitivity:** Animals respond quickly to stimuli and can move about from place to place. Plants respond to stimuli like light, water and gravity by growing slowly towards the stimulus, e.g. plants bend towards light.
- **Growth:** All living things grow.
- **Reproduction:** All living things reproduce, otherwise life would cease to exist.
- **Excretion:** All living things get rid of poisonous substances and waste. This is called excretion.
- **Cells**: All living things are made up of cells. Some organisms are made up of only one cell.

## STUDYING CELLS

Biologists study cells using a microscope. The parts of a typical microscope are shown here.

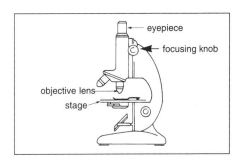

*Comparison of plant and animal cells*

Plant and animal cells have certain features in common. They also have features that are different.

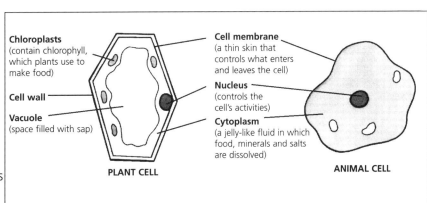

**Chloroplasts** (contain chlorophyll, which plants use to make food)

**Cell membrane** (a thin skin that controls what enters and leaves the cell)

**Cell wall**

**Nucleus** (controls the cell's activities)

**Vacuole** (space filled with sap)

**Cytoplasm** (a jelly-like fluid in which food, minerals and salts are dissolved)

**PLANT CELL**

**ANIMAL CELL**

| Plant cells | Animal cells |
|---|---|
| Contain chloroplasts | Do not contain chloroplasts |
| Have a cell wall | Do not have a cell wall |
| Have large vacuoles | Some have temporary vacuoles |

### Cell organisation

A **tissue** is a group of similar cells with a special function, e.g. muscle cells, nerve cells and blood cells.

An **organ** is a group of tissues that work together to perform a special function, e.g. a nose contains skin tissue, bone tissue and blood tissue; a leaf contains phloem and xylem tissue.

A **system** is a group of organs working together, e.g. the digestive system consists of intestines, stomach, oesophagus and other organs.

## CHAPTER 18. FEEDING AND DIGESTION

All living things need food for energy, for growth and repair, for movement and for protection against disease.

# BALANCED DIET

In order to stay healthy humans need a balanced diet.
**A balanced diet contains the right amount of all the food types essential for healthy living.**

| Type | Source | Function |
|---|---|---|
| **Carbohydrate** | Bread, potatoes and sugar | Quick release of energy |
| **Protein** | Meat, fish and vegetables | Growth and repair |
| **Fat** | Butter, oils and margarine | Slow release of energy |
| **Vitamins** | Vitamin C from oranges | Healthy skin and gums |
| | Vitamin D from milk | Strong bones and teeth |
| **Minerals** | Calcium from milk and eggs | Strong bones and teeth |
| | Iron from spinach and liver | Makes red blood cells |
| **Water** | Drinks and vegetables | Prevents dehydration |
| **Fibre** | Cereals and vegetables | Prevents constipation |

# FEEDING

Feeding for humans and most other animals involves the following processes.
- **Ingestion:** Food is taken into the mouth.
- **Digestion:** Food is broken up into soluble substances by the teeth and by digestive enzymes.
- **Absorption:** Soluble substances are absorbed into the bloodstream.
- **Assimilation:** The soluble products of digestion are reorganised and used for growth of new cells, for energy and for repair of tissues and organs.
- **Egestion:** Undigested material is got rid of (excreted) through the anus.

# THE DIGESTIVE SYSTEM

Food has to be broken up into smaller pieces before the body can use it. Food is broken up physically by the teeth and chemically by the digestive enzymes. Carbohydrates are broken up into glucose, proteins are broken up into amino acids, and fats are broken up into fatty acids and glycerol.

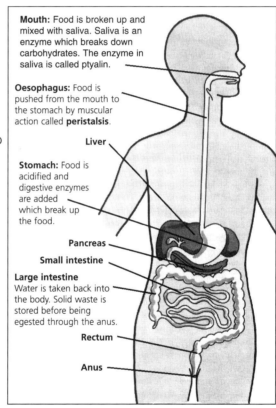

**Mouth:** Food is broken up and mixed with saliva. Saliva is an enzyme which breaks down carbohydrates. The enzyme in saliva is called ptyalin.

**Oesophagus:** Food is pushed from the mouth to the stomach by muscular action called **peristalsis**.

**Liver**

**Stomach:** Food is acidified and digestive enzymes are added which break up the food.

**Pancreas**

**Small intestine**

**Large intestine**
Water is taken back into the body. Solid waste is stored before being egested through the anus.

**Rectum**

**Anus**

**Digestive enzymes are biological catalysts which break down food.**

| | amylase | | maltase | |
|---|---|---|---|---|
| Example: starch | $\Rightarrow$ | maltose | $\Rightarrow$ | glucose |

## Enzyme action: starch into glucose

1. Add starch solution to each test-tube.
2. Add saliva to A, but not to B.
3. Place both test-tubes in a water bath at 37 °C for 15-20 minutes.
4. Use iodine to test B (no saliva) for starch. It turns blue-black.
5. Use Benedicts solution to test A for glucose. It turns red-orange.
6. Amylase present in saliva breaks down starch into glucose.

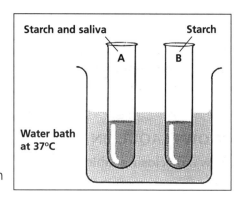

Starch and saliva     Starch

A    B

Water bath at 37°C

### End products of digestion

| Food type | End products of digestion |
|---|---|
| Carbohydrate | Simple sugars |
| Protein | Amino acids |
| Fats | Fatty acids and glycerol |

## TEETH

An adult has 32 teeth, 16 in the upper jaw and 16 in the lower jaw.
- **Incisors** are sharp for cutting food.
- **Canines** are cone-shaped for tearing food.
- **Premolars** are broad and bumpy for crushing food.
- **Molars** are large, broad and bumpy for crushing food.

### Tooth structure

- **Enamel** is the hard, non-living protective coating.
- **Dentine** is the soft living part.
- **Pulp cavity** contains living cells, nerves and blood.
- **Cement** holds the root firmly in place.

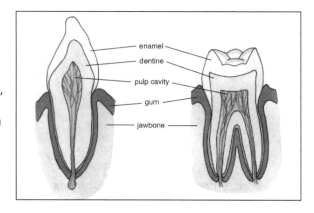

enamel
dentine
pulp cavity
gum
jawbone

### Tooth care

Tooth decay is caused by bacteria. Plaque is a build-up of sugar and bacteria. Plaque can be shown on teeth by a disclosing tablet, which turns plaque a dark red colour.

Tooth decay can be prevented by cleaning teeth regularly with a fluoride toothpaste and avoiding sugary foods.

# RESPIRATION

Respiration is a characteristic of all animal and plant cells. It is the release of energy from food  (usually glucose).

glucose   +   oxygen   $\Rightarrow$     carbon dioxide   +   water   +   energy

$C_6H_{12}O_6$   +   $6\ O_2$     $\Rightarrow$     $6\ CO_2$           +   $6\ H_2O$   +   energy

## BREATHING

Humans breathe by exchanging oxygen for carbon dioxide in the lungs. Fish breathe by extracting oxygen from water in their gills.

**Breathing is the process by which animals bring air or water into contact with their gaseous exchange surface.**

*The breathing system*

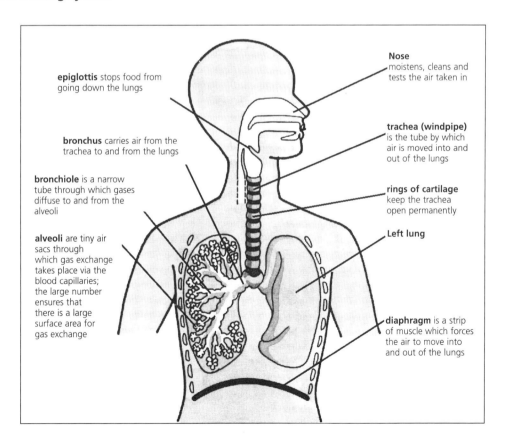

epiglottis stops food from
going down the lungs

bronchus carries air from the
trachea to and from the lungs

bronchiole is a narrow
tube through which gases
diffuse to and from the
alveoli

alveoli are tiny air
sacs through
which gas exchange
takes place via the
blood capillaries;
the large number
ensures that
there is a large
surface area for
gas exchange

**Nose**
moistens, cleans and
tests the air taken in

**trachea (windpipe)**
is the tube by which
air is moved into and
out of the lungs

**rings of cartilage**
keep the trachea
open permanently

**Left lung**

**diaphragm** is a strip
of muscle which forces
the air to move into
and out of the lungs

## Gas exchange in the alveoli

Oxygen passes through the walls of the alveoli and into the blood capillaries by **diffusion.** Carbon dioxide passes the other way by diffusion.

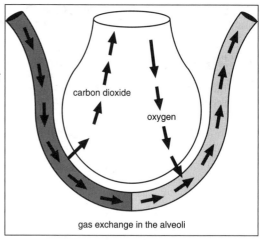

gas exchange in the alveoli

## Expired air contains more carbon dioxide than inspired air.

B takes longer to turn the limewater milky.

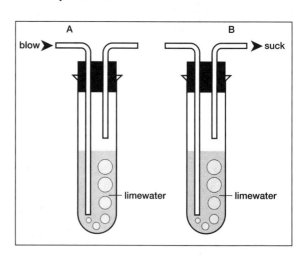

## Living organisms produce carbon dioxide.

The limewater turns milky.

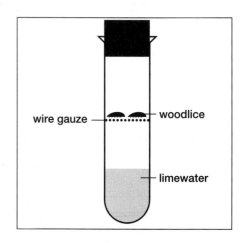

76

**Heat is produced during respiration.**

The temperature rises in A but not in B.

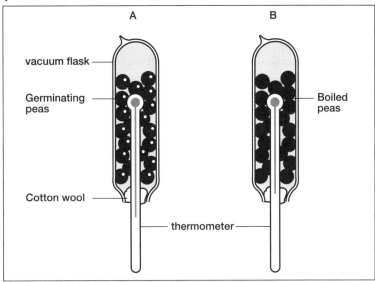

Dissolved foods, hormones, oxygen, carbon dioxide, unwanted waste and water are all transported around the body by blood.

**Circulation is the movement of blood around the body**.

# BLOOD

**Blood is a fluid consisting of blood cells and platelets suspended in a solution called plasma.**

*Composition of blood*

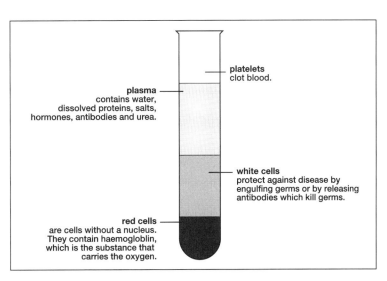

### Functions of the blood

Blood:

- **transports** food, oxygen, hormones, antibodies, carbon dioxide and unwanted substances like urea.
- **protects** against loss of fluid by clotting and also against disease by killing germs.
- **controls** the amounts of water and chemicals in the tissues.
- **regulates** body temperature.

## THE CIRCULATORY SYSTEM

- The **heart** pumps blood around the body.
- The heart is divided into **two sections** so that blood does not flow directly from one side to the other.
- **Arteries** carry blood away from the heart to the tissues. They have thick muscular walls.
- **Capillaries** carry blood through the tissues.
- **Veins** carry blood back to the heart. They have thinner walls and are wider than arteries.

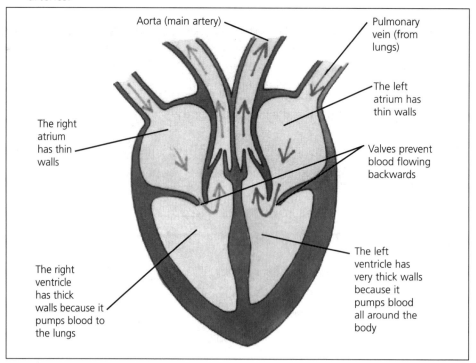

### Heart disease

Heart disease can be prevented by:

- regular exercise.
- a healthy diet.
- not smoking.

Humans produce waste products, such as carbon dioxide and urea during the day and at night. These waste products are the result of chemical reactions occurring in the cells of the body. The products are often poisonous and must be removed.

**Excretion is the removal of waste products produced during cell reactions from the body.**

# EXCRETORY ORGANS

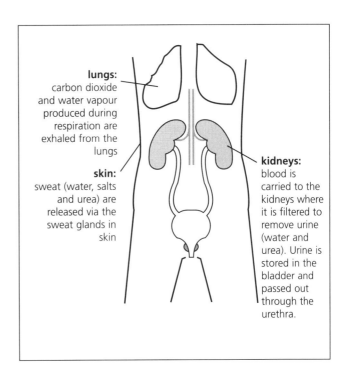

**lungs:** carbon dioxide and water vapour produced during respiration are exhaled from the lungs

**skin:** sweat (water, salts and urea) are released via the sweat glands in skin

**kidneys:** blood is carried to the kidneys where it is filtered to remove urine (water and urea). Urine is stored in the bladder and passed out through the urethra.

| Organ | Waste product |
|---|---|
| Lungs | $CO_2$ and $H_2O$ |
| Skin | Sweat |
| Kidneys | Urine |

Animal cells do not have cells made from cellulose to support them. Animal cells are supported by a framework called a skeleton. Some creatures, such as a lobster, have an outside skeleton **(exoskeleton)** while others, such as humans, have an inside skeleton **(endoskeleton).**

# FUNCTIONS OF THE SKELETON

**The Skeleton:**
- **supports** the body and maintains its shape.
- **protects** soft organs, e.g. brain, heart and lungs.
- **makes red blood cells** in the bone marrow.
- **enables us to move with the help of muscles.**

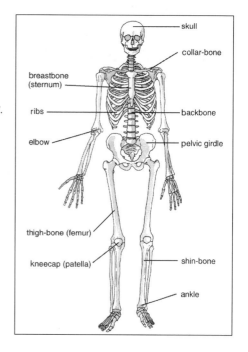

skull
collar-bone
breastbone (sternum)
ribs
backbone
elbow
pelvic girdle
thigh-bone (femur)
kneecap (patella)
shin-bone
ankle

## JOINTS

**A joint is the place where two bones move against each other.**

- **Ligaments** connect bone to bone. They are elastic and can be stretched.
- **Cartilage** is soft skeletal tissue which acts as a shock absorber between bones.
- **Synovial fluid** lubricates the joints and allows the bones to move easily.
- **Tendons** connect muscles to bones. They have little elasticity and cannot be stretched.

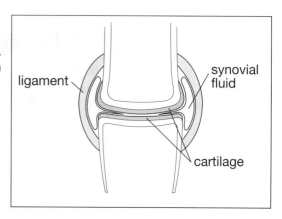

ligament
synovial fluid
cartilage

## Different types of joints

- **Ball and socket** allows movement in all directions, e.g. hips and shoulder.
- **Hinge** can bend in one direction only, e.g. knee and elbow.
- **Pivot** allows rotational movement, e.g. between head and backbone.
- **Gliding** allows sliding movement, e.g. in foot and hand and between the backbones.
- **Fused** has no movement, e.g. skull and pelvis.

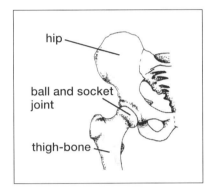

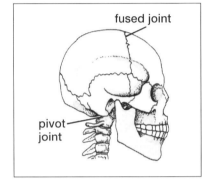

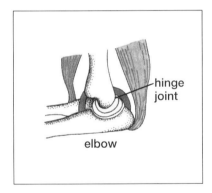

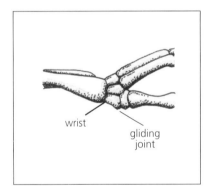

## MUSCLES

Bones are moved by the **contraction of muscles**. Usually, another muscle is used to return the bone to its original position. For this reason, muscles usually occur in antagonistic pairs which exert opposite forces.

**Antagonistic muscles are arranged in such a way that when they contract they produce opposite effects, e.g. the bending and straightening of the arm.**

### Bending the forearm

The arm is raised when the biceps contracts and the triceps relaxes. The arm is lowered when the biceps relaxes and the triceps contracts.

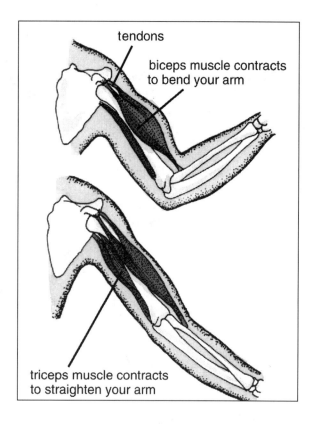

tendons

biceps muscle contracts to bend your arm

triceps muscle contracts to straighten your arm

## CHAPTER 23. SENSITIVITY AND CO-ORDINATION

## THE NERVOUS SYSTEM

The nervous system consists of the **brain, the spinal cord** and the **peripheral nerves** (nerves connected to the brain and the spinal cord). The function of the nervous system is to transmit messages rapidly to all parts of the body and to co-ordinate the body's responses.

**Nerves** are made up of millions of nerve cells called neurons. Messages travel very quickly along neurons as tiny electrical pulses.

**Sensory nerves** carry messages from the sense organ to the brain.

**Motor nerves** carry messages from the brain back to the sense organ.

### Sensory and motor functions

The sense organ receives a **stimulus**. A message is sent from the sense organ to the brain or spinal cord via a **sensory nerve.** The brain or spinal cord decides what to do, then sends a message along the **motor nerves** to the muscles and glands.

## THE EYE

The eye is a sense organ made up of receptors which receive light stimuli. The eyes are located in the cranium. An optic nerve connects each eye to the brain.

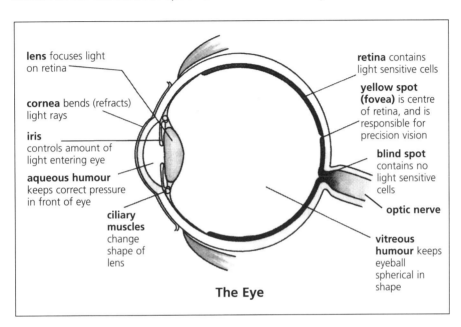

**lens** focuses light on retina

**cornea** bends (refracts) light rays

**iris** controls amount of light entering eye

**aqueous humour** keeps correct pressure in front of eye

**ciliary muscles** change shape of lens

**retina** contains light sensitive cells

**yellow spot (fovea)** is centre of retina, and is responsible for precision vision

**blind spot** contains no light sensitive cells

**optic nerve**

**vitreous humour** keeps eyeball spherical in shape

**The Eye**

### How does the eye work?

Light rays are bent (refracted) into the eye by the cornea and the lens. An image is formed on the retina. The light sensitive cells in the retina send a message to the brain, which produces an image.

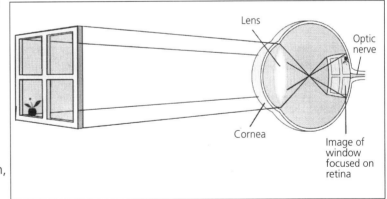

Lens

Optic nerve

Cornea

Image of window focused on retina

# THE ENDOCRINE (HORMONE) SYSTEM

**Hormones** are chemical messengers which are produced in the endocrine glands.
Hormones are released directly into the bloodstream. The message is not carried as quickly as a nerve impulse, but has a longer effect.

**Insulin** is produced in the **pancreas**. Insulin controls the amount of sugar in the bloodstream. Lack of insulin causes **diabetes**.

**Oestrogen** is a female **sex hormone**. It controls sex characteristics and the menstrual cycle.

**Progesterone** prepares the body for pregnancy.

**Testosterone** is the principle male sex hormone. It controls sex characteristics.

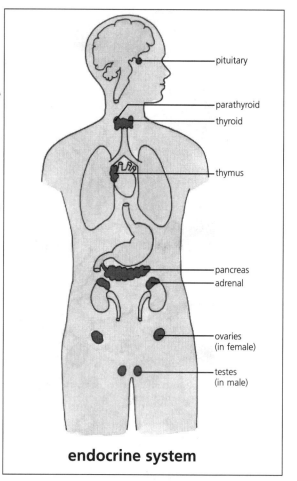

**endocrine system**

---

**CHAPTER 24. REPRODUCTION**

## SEXUAL REPRODUCTION

**Sexual reproduction is the production of offspring by a male and a female.**

The male produces a male sex cell (gamete) called a **sperm**. Sperm are produced in the **testes**. The female produces a female sex cell (gamete) called an **egg** (ovum). Eggs are produced in the **ovaries**. The production of eggs is called **ovulation**.

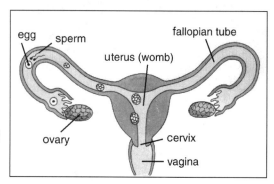

The fusion of the sperm with the egg is called **fertilisation.**

## REPRODUCTIVE ORGANS

The diagrams below show the male and female reproductive organs.

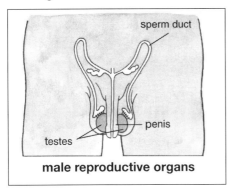

**male reproductive organs**

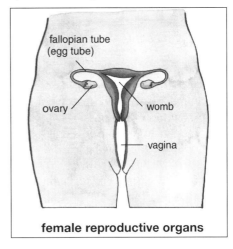

**female reproductive organs**

### What happens during reproduction ?

**Sexual intercourse** takes place when the male inserts his penis into the female's vagina.

**Insemination** occurs when sperm are released into the vagina. The sperm travel from the vagina up through the womb and into the **fallopian tubes.** If a fertile egg is present, the sperm may **fertilise** the egg. At this stage the female is **pregnant**.

The fertilised egg starts to **subdivide** into more and more cells. This group of cells, called an embryo, moves down the fallopian tube and is **implanted** (attached) into the soft lining of the womb. During the next **36 weeks** or so the embryo develops.

The **umbilical cord** connects the embryo to the **placenta**. The placenta is a filter which allows food and oxygen to pass from the mother to the embryo, and carbon dioxide and other wastes to pass from the embryo to the mother.

**Birth** occurs some time after the amnion (water sac) bursts. The baby usually comes out head first. The umbilical cord is cut and the placenta (afterbirth) comes out. Milk is produced in the breasts to feed the baby.

# THE MENSTRUAL CYCLE

Every twenty-eight days or so a woman's body goes through a series of changes in preparation for pregnancy. When the woman is not pregnant, the lining of the womb breaks down for the first five days or so. It then starts to build up again in preparation for a possible pregnancy. Pregnancy is only possible during ovulation (thirteenth, fourteenth and fifteenth days). This is called the **fertile period**.

If pregnancy occurs, the embryo attaches itself to the wall of the womb. If no pregnancy occurs, the lining is not needed and starts to break down again. The cycle begins during **puberty** (9 -14 years) and continues until the **menopause** or 'change of life' (45 - 55 years).

MENSTRUAL CYCLE

IF FERTILISATION DOES NOT OCCUR

MENSTRUATION LINING BREAKS DOWN

WOMB LINING BUILDS UP AGAIN

OVULATION EGG RELEASED

FERTILE PERIOD

LINING STAYS BUILT UP IF FERTILISATION OCCURS

# CONTRACEPTION

**Contraception is a practise or device that prevents fertilisation of an egg by a sperm.**

- **Rhythm method**: When the egg is released from the ovary, the woman's body temperature rises by about 1 °C. If the woman avoids intercourse at this time, fertilisation will not take place. This method involves the constant measurement of body temperature and can lead to error.
- The **contraceptive pill**: The pill is a dose of hormones that fools the woman's body into believing fertilisation has taken place. As a result, no egg is released. Overuse can cause health problems in some women.
- **Condom**: This is a rubber sheath which is placed over the penis before intercourse. It catches the semen during ejaculation.
- **Sterilisation**: Males are sterilised by having their sperm ducts cut and tied. Females are sterilised by having their fallopian tubes cut and tied. Sterilisation is usually irreversible.

**Importance of plants:**
- a source of oxygen.
- the start of all food chains.
- can be a source of food.
- a source of materials such as timber, cotton, linen and paper.
- a source of medicines.
- leisure and aesthetic values.

# PLANT STRUCTURE

The main parts of a plant are the root, the stem, the leaf, the flower and the fruit.

**Leaf:**
- makes food by photosynthesis.
- allows carbon dioxide to move in and oxygen to move out of the plant.
- releases water from the plant.
- can be a food store, e.g. lettuce and cabbage leaves.

**Stem:**
- carries water and minerals up from the roots to the leaves.
- carries food down from the leaves to the rest of the plant.
- can be a food store, e.g. celery and rhubarb stems.

**Roots:**
- absorb water and minerals from the soil.
- anchor the plant to the ground.
- can be food stores, e.g. carrot and turnip roots.

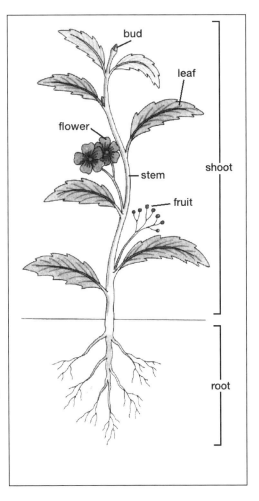

# PLANT CELLS

## Transporting tissue

**Phloem cells** carry food down from the leaves to the rest of the plant.
**Xylem cells** carry water and minerals up from the roots to the leaves.

## Growing tissue

Cambium cells grow into new xylem and phloem cells.

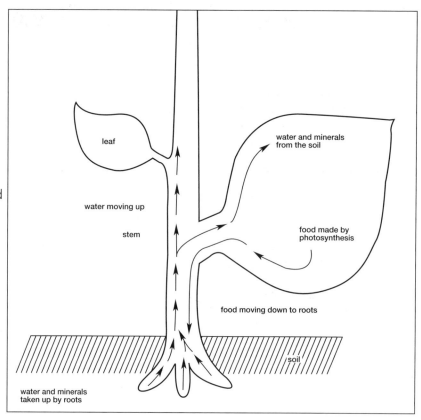

leaf

water and minerals from the soil

water moving up

stem

food made by photosynthesis

food moving down to roots

soil

water and minerals taken up by roots

## Photosynthetic tissue

Chloroplasts present in the green cells in leaves contain chlorophyll which helps to make food.

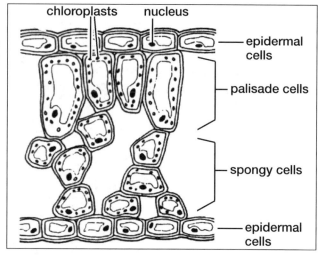

chloroplasts    nucleus

epidermal cells

palisade cells

spongy cells

epidermal cells

## Plants make food by photosynthesis.

Plants make **glucose** from carbon dioxide and water by using the energy from the sun and a catalyst called chlorophyll. Glucose can be used as energy, stored as starch, converted into protein or used to make cell walls.

Most **leaves** are broad, flat and thin. This allows the maximum amount of light to be absorbed and also allows carbon dioxide to be taken in quickly.

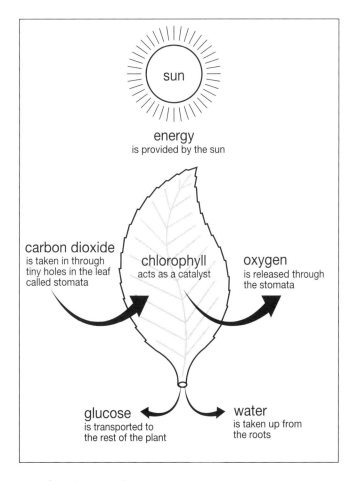

The word equation for photosynthesis is

**carbon dioxide + water + sunlight + chlorophyll $\Rightarrow$ glucose + oxygen**

The balanced chemical equation is

**$6\ CO_2 + 6\ H_2O\ =\ C_6H_{12}O_6\ +\ 6\ O_2$**

### Experiment: Testing a leaf for starch

1. Boil the leaf in water to kill the leaf and break open the cells.
2. Boil the leaf in alcohol to remove the chlorophyll.
3. Rinse with water to soften the leaf.
4. Add iodine to the leaf.
5. If starch is present, the leaf turns black.

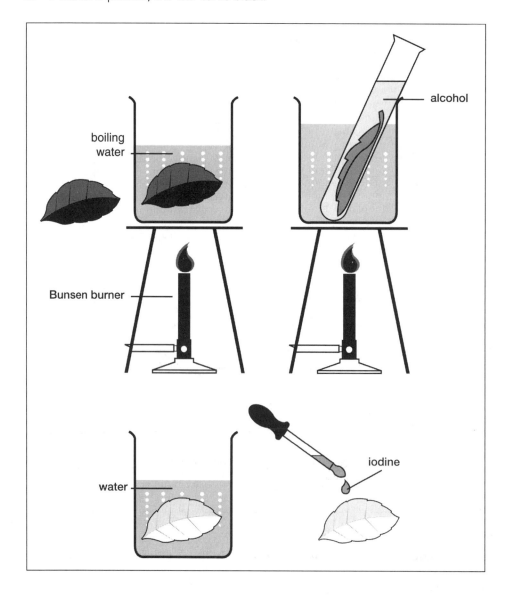

## Conditions necessary for photosynthesis

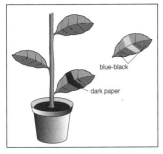

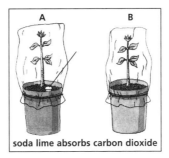

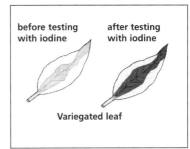

Variegated leaf

| Light | Carbon dioxide | Chlorophyll |
|---|---|---|
| Destarch plant | Destarch plant | Destarch a variegated leaf |
| Cover part of the leaf | Remove carbon dioxide using soda lime | Remove the chlorophyll |
| Leave for 6-8 hours | Leave for 6-8 hours | Leave for 6-8 hours |
| Test for starch | Test for starch | Test for starch |
| Covered part has no starch | No carbon dioxide, no starch | Part with no chlorophyll has no starch |

## Oxygen is given off during photosynthesis

1. Allow gas to collect in the test-tube.
2. Test the gas with a glowing splint.
3. Oxygen re-lights a glowing splint.

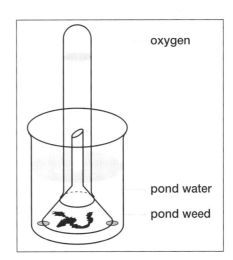

### *Nitrogen is necessary for plant growth*

1. Solution A is a complete growing solution.
2. Solution B is deficient in nitrogen.
3. Allow the solutions to stand for approximately 2 weeks in the light.
4. The leaves in B are stunted and are yellow.

**Plants need nitrogen, phosphorous, potassium and other trace elements for growth.**

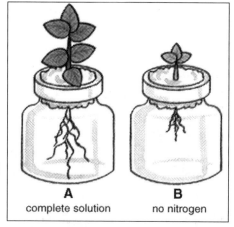

**A**
complete solution

**B**
no nitrogen

## CHAPTER 27. TRANSPORT IN PLANTS

Water and minerals flow up from the roots to the rest of the plant. Food made in the leaves is carried to other parts of the plant.

The flow of water from the roots to the leaves is called the transpiration stream.

**Transpiration is the loss of water from the leaves of the plant.**

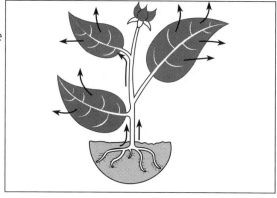

The factors that effect transpiration are wind, sunlight, humidity, temperature and the amount of water in the soil.
The rate of transpiration is increased by high winds, bright sunlight, low humidity, high temperature, high water content in soil and the absence of thinner cuticle.

# MOVEMENT OF WATER IN PLANTS

## Absorption of water by roots

1. Leave A and B for about a week.
2. The level in A falls due to the uptake of water by the roots.

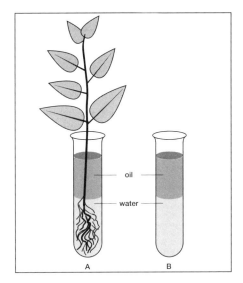

## Transpiration in plants

[Diagram 27.3]
1. Place the growing plant in soil.
2. Seal off the roots by tying polythene bag to stem.
3. Leave the plant in a warm place for several hours.
4. Test the droplets of water on the inside of the polythene with cobalt chloride paper.
5. The cobalt chloride paper turns from blue to pink.

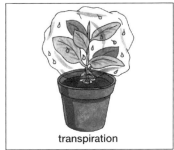

transpiration

# FOOD TRANSPORT

Food is transported from the leaf by the phloem vessels to all parts of the plant.

Transport of food is affected by temperature and the amount of oxygen.

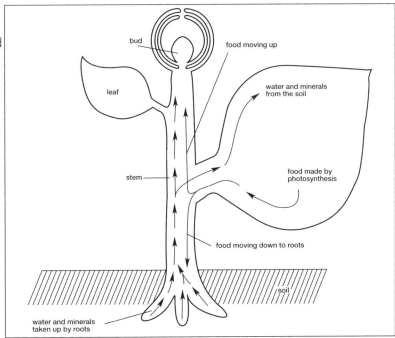

**Tropism is the response of a plant to a stimulus.**

**Phototropism is the growth response of a plant to light.**

1. Leave the plant for a few days with light shining through the hole.
2. The plant grows towards the light.

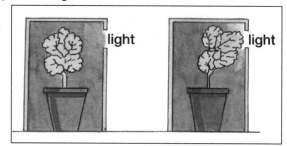

**Geotropism is the growth response of plant to gravity.**

1. Plant some bean seeds, some the right way up, some upside down and some sideways.
2. No matter which way they are planted, the roots grow down and the stem grows up.

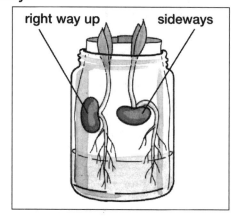

# CHAPTER 29. PLANT REPRODUCTION

**Asexual reproduction** involves only one parent. No fusion of gametes (sex cells) is involved. **All offspring are identical to the parent**. Examples include mushroom spores, daffodil bulbs, crocus corms, potato tubers, iris rhizomes, strawberry runners, and all cuttings and graftings.

**Sexual reproduction** occurs when a male gamete (sex cell) fuses with a female gamete (sex cell).

# FLOWER

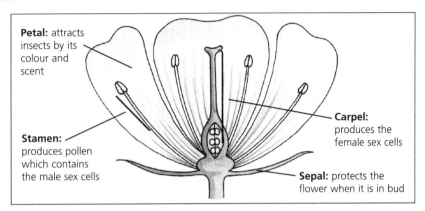

**Petal:** attracts insects by its colour and scent

**Stamen:** produces pollen which contains the male sex cells

**Carpel:** produces the female sex cells

**Sepal:** protects the flower when it is in bud

## Pollination

**Pollination is the transfer of pollen from the anther to the stigma.**

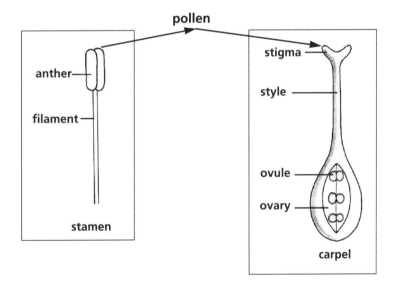

pollen

anther

filament

stamen

stigma

style

ovule

ovary

carpel

## Methods of pollination
- Insect:  Bees and other insects carry pollen from one flower to another.
- Wind:  The wind blows pollen from one flower to another.

## Differences between insect- and wind-pollinated flowers

| Part of flower | Insect-pollinated | Wind-pollinated |
|---|---|---|
| Petals | Large, coloured, scented | Often green |
| Stamens | Inside flower | Hang outside flower |
| Pollen grains | Large | Small |
| Stigma | Small, inside flower | Feathery, hang outside |

**Fertilisation occurs when the male gamete fuses with the female sex cell.**

**Fertilisation occurs after pollination.**

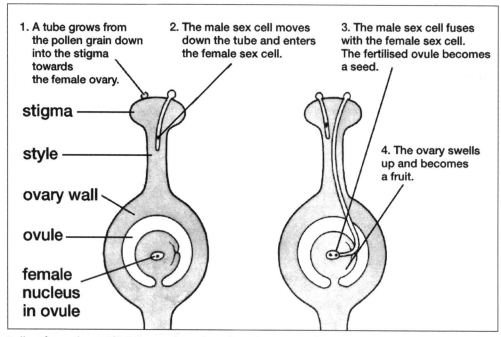

1. A tube grows from the pollen grain down into the stigma towards the female ovary.

2. The male sex cell moves down the tube and enters the female sex cell.

3. The male sex cell fuses with the female sex cell. The fertilised ovule becomes a seed.

4. The ovary swells up and becomes a fruit.

stigma

style

ovary wall

ovule

female nucleus in ovule

Pollen from the anther is transferred to the stigma. A tube grows from the pollen grain down into the stigma and towards the female ovary.
The male sex cell moves down the tube and enters the female sex cell. The male sex cell then fuses with the female sex cell. The fertilised ovule becomes a **seed**. The ovary swells up and becomes a fruit.

### Seed dispersal

- **Wind:** Dandelions and thistles have 'parachutes' which float in the wind.
- **Animal:** Burdock seeds stick to animals and are carried away. Berries are eaten by animals and are passed out later.
- **Self-dispersal:** Peas burst out of their pods.
- **Water:** Water lilies produce seeds which can float away.

## Germination

Germination is the growth of the seed into a new plant.

Air, water and heat are conditions necessary for germination.

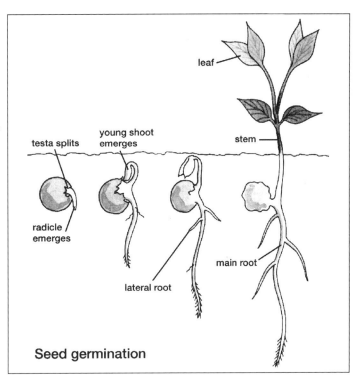

Seed germination

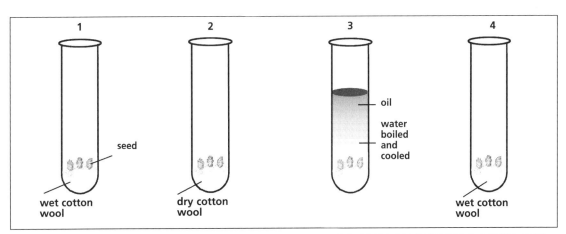

| Test-tube 1 | Test-tube 2 | Test-tube 3 | Test-tube 4 |
|---|---|---|---|
| 20 °C | 20 °C | 20 °C | - 5 °C |
| Wet cotton wool | Dry cotton wool | Water, boiled and cooled | Wet cotton wool |
| Germinates | Does not germinate | Does not germinate | Does not germinate |
| Has air, water and heat | Has no water | Has no air | Has no heat |

## Life cycle of a flowering plant

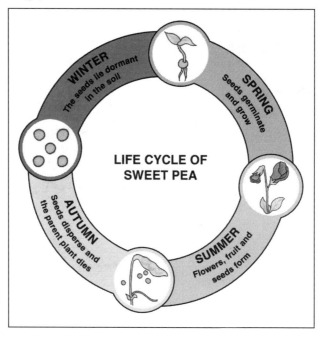

# HABITATS

A habitat is the place where an organism lives, e.g. a woodland, a sea-shore and a pond.

**Ecology** is the study of the relationships between plants and animals in their environment.

An **ecosystem** is the combination of the animal and plant community with their environment.

### Feeding relationships

Energy is transferred from the sun to the plants. The plants produce food by photosynthesis. Plants transfer this food energy to animals.

**Producers** are plants that make food by photosynthesis.

**Consumers** are organisms that cannot make food, e.g. animals, fungi and most bacteria.

**Herbivores** are animals that eat plants, e.g. cows and sheep.

**Carnivores** are animals that eat other animals, e.g. foxes.

**Omnivores** are animals that eat both plants and other animals, e.g. humans.

**Decomposers** are organisms that break down dead animal and plant matter, e.g. bacteria and fungi.

## *Food chain*

The food chain is a sequence of organisms in which each organism provides food for the next organism.

Plants form the first link in a food chain: **grass** $\Rightarrow$ **rabbit** $\Rightarrow$ **fox.**

Food chains are usually written as :

| | | | |
|---|---|---|---|
| **producer** | $\Rightarrow$ **primary consumer** | $\Rightarrow$ **secondary consumer** | $\Rightarrow$ **tertiary consumer** |
| **first trophic level** | $\Rightarrow$ **second trophic level** | $\Rightarrow$ **third trophic level** | $\Rightarrow$ **fourth trophic level** |
| pond weed | $\Rightarrow$ tadpole | $\Rightarrow$ beetle | $\Rightarrow$ pike |

**Trophic level** is the position of an organism in a food chain.

**Food web** is a number of interconnecting food chains.

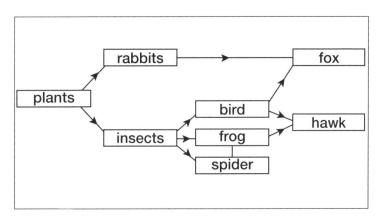

## Pyramid of numbers

A primary consumer needs many small plants to feed on. A secondary consumer is usually a larger animal than a primary consumer and needs more food to feed on.

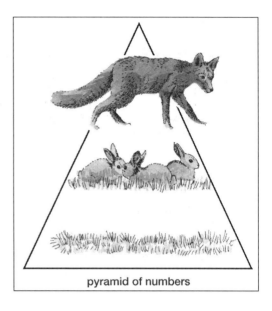

pyramid of numbers

### Adaptation

Plants and animals adapt special features which enable them to survive in their environments.

Squirrels have many special features including sharp teeth for eating nuts, and large eyes at the side of their head which enable them to see over a wide viewing range.

Flowers have attractive colours and scent which attract insects for pollination.

### Competition

Animals and plants compete with each other for many things including light, food, water, territory, shelter and for partners.

### Interdependence

- Animals and plants depend on each other for survival.
- Plants depend on animals for pollination and for seed dispersal.
- Dead animals and their waste products provide fertile soil for plants.
- Animals produce carbon dioxide which is necessary for photosynthesis.
- Plants produce oxygen during photosynthesis which helps animals to breathe.

### Balance of nature

The feeding relationships in an ecosystem are finely balanced. Too many or too few of one species can alter the number of another species, e.g. too many foxes in a habitat would mean fewer rabbits. If the number of foxes was lowered, the population of rabbits would increase. This larger rabbit population would then eat more plants, and upset the balance of nature.

### Deforestation

Deforestation is the removal of large areas of trees. Removal of trees leads to a loss of oxygen, increases the amount of carbon dioxide and can also cause erosion or desertification.

**Desertification** is the cutting down of large forest areas, resulting
in large areas of dry dusty soil.

## Conservation

Conservation is the management of our natural resources by protection and
preservation.

## Pollution

Pollution is any undesirable change in our environment caused by human activities.

- **Water pollution** is the introduction of anything into water which alters any of its
  beneficial uses, e.g. sailing, fishing and drinking.
- **Atmospheric pollution** is the introduction of small suspended solids or poisonous
  liquids and gases into the air.
- **Acid rain** is caused by an increase in the pH of normal rain-water by the introduction
  of sulphur dioxide and the oxides of nitrogen into the air.

## The greenhouse effect

Certain gases in the air absorb uv radiation, which causes an increase in the temperature
of the earth. Carbon dioxide, methane and CFCs are some examples of 'greenhouse
gases'.

## The ozone layer

A layer of ozone gas protects us from the harmful effects of radiation from the sun.
Some gases, CFCs in particular, have created a hole in the ozone layer.

## CHAPTER 31. HABITAT STUDY

A **pooter** is an instrument used to
collect small insects by sucking them up.

using a pooter

suck

A **pitfall trap** is used to collect small insects as they walk along the ground.

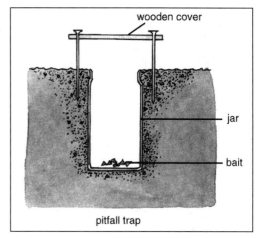

pitfall trap

A **Tullgren funnel** is used to collect small animals and micro-organisms from soil or leaf litter.

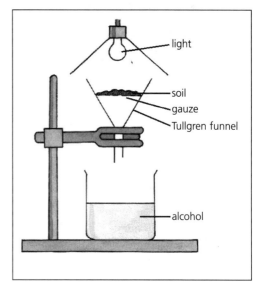

A **quadrat** is a square frame, which is thrown a number of times at random in a habitat. It is used to estimate the number of plants in a habitat.

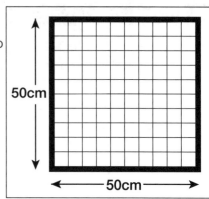

A **line transect** is used to study plant variations from one part of a habitat to another. A piece of twine

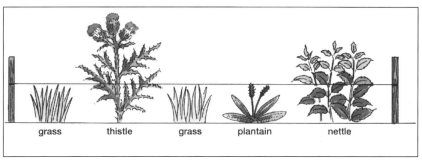

or rope is stretched across a habitat. The name and height of each plant touching the rope at regular intervals (1 metre) is recorded.

## CHAPTER 32. SOIL

Soil particles are formed by the weathering of rocks over thousands of years. Soil is important because it acts as a store for chemicals which plants can use.

Soil consists of different types and sizes of particles.

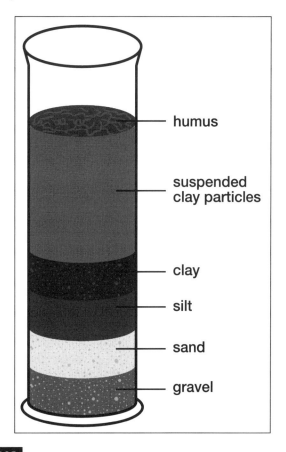

## Finding the percentage of water in soil

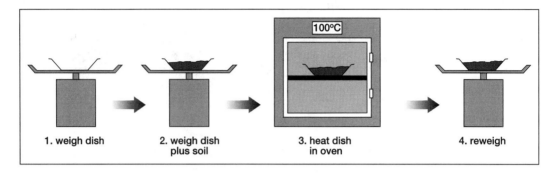

1. weigh dish
2. weigh dish plus soil
3. heat dish in oven
4. reweigh

1. Weigh a sample of soil.
2. Heat it in an oven at 100 °C for at least 1 hour.
3. Remove the dish from the oven, cool and reweigh.
4. Re-heat until no further change in weight occurs.

5. Percentage of water $= \dfrac{\text{loss in weight}}{\text{original weight}}$

## Finding the percentage of humus in soil

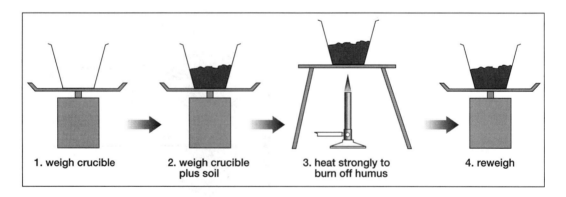

1. weigh crucible
2. weigh crucible plus soil
3. heat strongly to burn off humus
4. reweigh

1. Weigh a sample of dry soil.
2. Heat the sample strongly to burn off the humus.
3. Cool the sample and reweigh it.

4. Percentage of humus $= \dfrac{\text{loss in weight}}{\text{original weight}}$

## Finding the percentage of air in soil

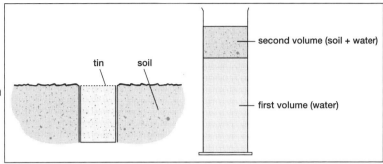

tin    soil

second volume (soil + water)

first volume (water)

1. Measure the volume of the tin (50 cm$^3$).
2. Screw the tin into the soil. Remove a full tin of soil from the ground.
3. Fill a graduated cylinder with water up to the half-way mark (50 cm$^3$).
4. Add the soil to the water.
5. Note the new volume (80 cm$^3$).
6. Percentage of air $= \dfrac{\text{decrease in volume}}{\text{total volume}} = \dfrac{20\ \text{cm}^3}{100\ \text{cm}^3} \times 100\ \% = 20\ \%$

## Comparing the drainage of sandy soil and clay soil

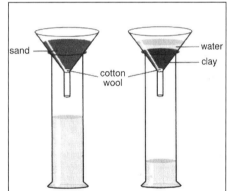

sand    water    clay    cotton wool

1. At the same time, pour equal volumes of water through the sand and the clay.
2. Sandy soil drains quicker than clay soil.

## Testing the pH of soil

Test the pH of soil with universal indicator paper.

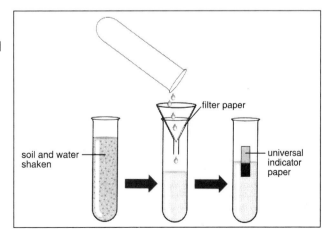

filter paper    soil and water shaken    universal indicator paper

*Showing micro-organisms in soil*

1. Place a sample of soil on a sterile petri dish containing nutrient agar.
2. Seal a second sterile dish without soil.
3. Incubate at 37 °C for 72 hours.
4. Shiny patches of bacteria and fungi will appear as colonies on the dish which contained the soil.

# MICRO-ORGANISMS

Micro-organisms are very small organisms. Some are beneficial to humans while others can be harmful.

Viruses are micro-organisms that multiply only in living cells by making replicas of themselves. Viruses cause influenza, colds, polio, AIDS, and many other illnesses.

Bacteria are single cells that can reproduce very quickly. Harmful bacteria cause diseases such as pneumonia and tuberculosis.

Many fungi, such as mushrooms, are not micro-organisms. Fungi have no chlorophyll and cannot produce food by photosynthesis.

*Beneficial and harmful bacteria and fungi*

| Beneficial bacteria | Harmful bacteria | Beneficial fungi | Harmful fungi |
|---|---|---|---|
| Decompose dead matter<br>Produce antibiotics<br><br>Used to make vinegar and yoghurt | Cause tooth decay<br><br>Cause diseases<br><br>Spoil food | Used as food (mushrooms)<br>Produce antibiotics<br><br>Used to make alcohol and bread (yeast) | Can be poisonous<br><br>Cause diseases (athletes foot)<br>Spoil food (moulds) |

# APPLIED SCIENCE

**CHAPTER 33. EARTH SCIENCE**

## THE UNIVERSE

The universe is made up of all the matter that exists. Earth is a very small part of the universe. It is part of a galaxy called the milky way.

A **galaxy** is a group of stars held together by gravity.

The **solar system** is the sun and the nine planets orbiting around it. The nine **planets** are Earth, Mercury, Venus, Mars, Jupiter, Saturn, Uranus, Neptune and Pluto.

The **sun** contains most of the mass of the solar system. The gravitational force of the sun keeps the planets moving around it.

The **milky way** is spiral in shape and contains millions of stars held together by gravity.

### Earth - the blue planet

Earth is the only planet in the solar system known to be capable of sustaining life. The earth looks blue because three-quarters of the earth's surface is water.

The average temperature of the earth is 15 °C. The earth moves around the sun. The sun keeps the earth warm and provides energy for photosynthesis.

**Comparison of the earth with the moon and Mars**

|  | Earth | Moon | Mars |
|---|---|---|---|
| **Size (diameter/km)** | 12750 | 3500 | 6750 |
| **Distance from sun (million km)** | 150 | 150 | 2228 |
| **Gravity** | 9.8 | 1.6 | 3.6 |
| **Temperature (°C)** | 15 | - 60 | - 50 |
| **Atmosphere** | 78% nitrogen 21% oxygen | None  9 | 5% carbon dioxide 3% nitrogen 2% argon |
| **Planetary moons** | One – the moon | None | Two |

## The calendar

A day is the time that the earth takes to rotate about its axis.

A year is the time that the earth takes to move one complete orbit around the sun.

The **seasons** are caused because the earth is tilted at an angle of 23 °C to its orbit around the sun. When tilted towards the sun it is summer; when tilted away from the sun it is winter.

A **solar eclipse** takes place when the moon is in a straight line between the sun and the earth.

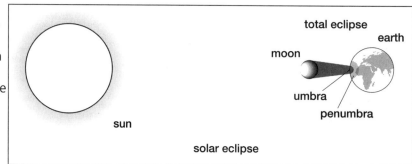

solar eclipse

## Life cycle of a star

Stars are formed when dust clouds are pulled together.
Stars burn for thousands of years with no change in size.
Nuclear reactions in the sun will cause it to expand outwards and form a red giant. The red giant will get so big that it will spread out as far as Mars. The outer layers will use up their fuel and cool, leaving a small hot core called a white dwarf. The white dwarf will slowly die out.

**Formation** ⇒ **Stable** ⇒ **Growth** ⇒ **Death**

## The moon

The moon is a satellite of the earth.

**Phases of the moon**

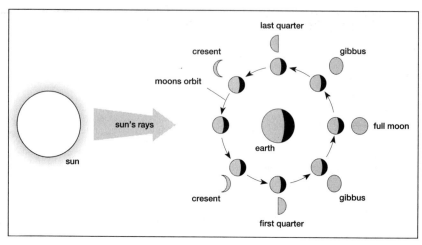

A **lunar eclipse** takes place when the earth is in a straight line between the sun and the moon.

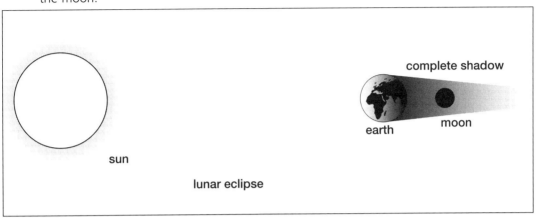

complete shadow

moon

earth

sun

lunar eclipse

## Tides

The gravitational pull of the sun pulls the waters in the oceans towards it, causing the water to rise.

The moon is closer to earth and has a greater pull on the oceans. As the earth rotates, the pull of the moon causes the rise and fall of tides twice a day.

**High tides** (spring tides) occur when the gravitational pull of the sun and moon add to each other. This occurs when the sun, the moon and the earth are in a straight line.

**Low tides** (neap tides) occur when the gravitational pull of the sun and the moon cancel each other out. This happens when the sun and the moon are at right angles to each other.

Low

High EARTH High MOON

Low

## WEATHER

### *Water in the atmosphere*

Radiation from the sun heats the land and the seas. Radiated heat from the land and the seas heats the atmosphere. Water from the earth evaporates and condenses to form clouds. Evaporation and condensation are dependent on temperature and wind.

## Clouds are water vapour containing tiny drops of condensed water.

When the air cools more water vapour is converted into drops. When the drops get bigger rain falls.

Clouds also form when hot moist air rises. As the pressure drops the hot air expands and cools to form rain.

Different types of clouds

- **Stratocumulus** are low-level clouds that cause drizzle.
- **Cumulus** are thick billowing clouds that give light rain. They usually indicate fine weather.
- **Nimbostratus** are grey-black, layered clouds that give persistent rain.
- **Cirrus** are long white clouds. As they become thicker they indicate the start of a warm front.
- **Fog** occurs at night or early in the morning. It is caused by the cooling of very small drops of water vapour in the air just above the ground.
- **Frost** occurs on cold clear nights when water vapour in the air condenses on to the ground as a light coating of ice.

## *Measurement of humidity*

When the air holds as much water as possible it is saturated. Humidity is the amount of water compared to its saturation point.

Humidity is related to temperature. It is measured using a **hygrometer.**

## *Measuring humidity*

1. Use a hygrometer (wet bulb thermometer).
2. Note the temperature difference.
3. If the temperatures are close to each other, the humidity is high. If they are different, the humidity is low

## *Measurement of atmospheric pressure*

The **mercury barometer** is a long glass tube sealed at one end, with the other dipped into a dish of mercury.

Atmospheric pressure is measured by measuring the vertical height from the surface of mercury in the dish to the top of the mercury in the tube. Normal atmospheric pressure supports a column of mercury 76 cm high.

Pressure is measured in **pascals**
(1 Pa = 1 N/m$^2$).

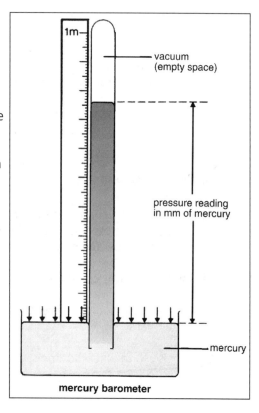

**mercury barometer**

The **aneroid barometer** is a partially evacuated sealed metal box connected to a system of levers. As the pressure increases the sides of the box move in and push a pointer on a scale.

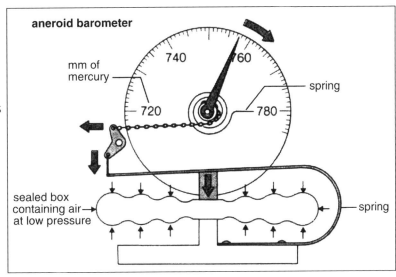

aneroid barometer

mm of mercury

740  760

720  780

spring

sealed box containing air → at low pressure

spring

**Altimeters** are special types of aneroid barometer used to measure height above sea-level. As the altitude increases, the pressure decreases.

## Properties of gases

**Boyle's law: for a fixed mass of gas at constant temperature, the pressure is inversely proportional to the volume, i.e. P x V = constant**.

1. Record the pressure and the volume.
2. Increase the pressure and re-measure the volume.
3. Repeat for four or five readings.
4. Each time, pressure multiplied by volume equals a constant value, i.e. **P x V = constant**.

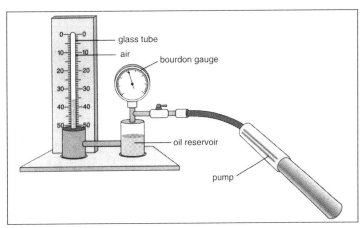

glass tube

air

bourdon gauge

oil reservoir

pump

Example: A balloon contains 3000 cm³ of air at a pressure of 5 Pa. Calculate the volume of air in the balloon at 15 Pa.

$$P_1V_1 \quad = \quad P_2V_2$$

$$5 \text{ Pa} \times 3000 \text{ cm}^3 \quad = \quad 15 \text{ Pa} \times V_2$$

$$V_2 \quad = \quad \frac{5 \times 3000}{15} \text{ cm}^3 \quad = \quad 1000 \text{ cm}^3$$

**Charles' law: for a fixed mass of gas at constant pressure, the Kelvin temperature is directly proportional to the volume, i.e.**

$$\frac{V_1}{T_1} = \frac{V_2}{T_2}$$

Example: A balloon has a volume of 870 cm$^3$ at 17 $^{\circ}$C. Calculate the volume of the balloon at a temperature of 30 $^{\circ}$C, when the pressure remains constant.

$$\frac{V_1}{T_1} = \frac{V_2}{T_2} \quad \textit{(Always convert } ^{\circ}\textit{C to K, 0 } ^{\circ}\textit{C} = 273 \textit{ K)}$$

$$\frac{870 \text{ cm}^3}{290 \text{ K}} = \frac{V_2}{303 \text{ K}} \quad (17°C = 290K; \ 30°C = 303K)$$

$$V_2 = \frac{870 \times 303}{290} \text{ cm}^3 = 909 \text{ cm}^3$$

## *Transfer of energy*

The sun heats the earth by radiation. Most of this heat is radiated back into space, while some of the heat is absorbed by gases in the atmosphere.

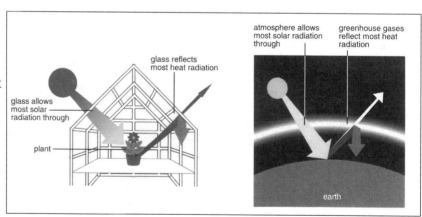

This keeps the earth warm: the atmosphere acts as a blanket. Gases, such as carbon dioxide, water vapour and methane, which absorb heat radiation in this way are called **greenhouse gases**.

### Measurement of wind speed

The anemometer measures wind speed by measuring the speed of a set of rotating cups attached to a shaft.

### Measurement of temperature

A maximum and minimum thermometer is used to record the temperature range over a fixed time.

### Measurement of rainfall

Rainfall is measured using a **rain gauge**. A rain gauge has a funnel which drains into a storage container. The rainfall is measured in millimetres.

### High pressure and low pressure

An area of **high pressure** is an area of stable high pressure air. This causes the clouds to sink and turn to water vapour, making the sky **clear and sunny**.

An area of **low pressure** is an area of rotating unstable low pressure air. This is caused when warm air moves over cold air. The warm moist air is cooled by the cold air and turns to rain. The sky is **cloudy and rainy** in low pressure areas.

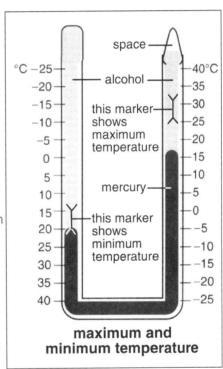

**maximum and minimum temperature**

# SOIL AND PLANT NUTRITION

Plants are usually grown in soil, which provides water and nutrients. Water is transported from the soil up to the leaves where photosynthesis takes place. Food made by photosynthesis is transported to the rest of the plant. Energy is released from the food during respiration.

## Soil structure

Soil is usually described as sandy, clay or loam. Loam is a mixture of sand and clay, and also contains humus which aerates the soil.

Soil contains soil particles, humus, water, plant nutrients, air and living organisms. It is also full of living animals. Earthworms help to aerate, fertilise and drain the soil.

## Plant nutrients

Plants need nitrogen, phosphorous, potassium, calcium, magnesium, manganese, iron, molybdenum, sulphur, boron, zinc and copper for healthy growth.

| Nutrient | Function | Deficiency |
|---|---|---|
| Nitrogen (N) | Healthy leaves | Small yellow leaves; stunted growth |
| Phosphorous (P) | Healthy roots | Reddish leaves; stunted growth; poor roots |
| Potassium (K) | Good flowers and fruit | Poor flowers and fruit; poor resistance to disease |

### Showing the deficiency of nitrogen, phosphorous and potassium on plant growth

1.  Place similar seedlings in a growing medium.
2.  Add standard nutrient solution to A.
3.  Add standard nutrient solution without nitrogen to B.
4.  Add standard nutrient solution without phosphorous to C.
5.  Add standard nutrient solution without potassium to D.

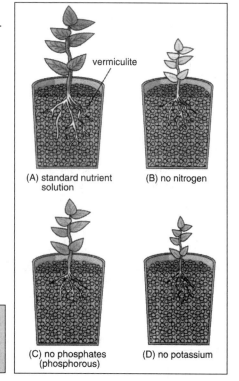

(A) standard nutrient solution

(B) no nitrogen

(C) no phosphates (phosphorous)

(D) no potassium

Results after 1-2 weeks:

| A | Standard solution | Normal growth |
|---|---|---|
| B | Solution without nitrogen | Small yellow leaves |
| C | Solution without phosphorous | Stunted growth |
| D | Solution without potassium | Stunted growth |

## Finding the percentage of water in soil

1. Weigh a sample of soil.
2. Heat it in an oven at 100 °C for at least 1 hour.
3. Remove the dish from the oven, cool and reweigh.
4. Re-heat until no further change in weight occurs.
5. Percentage of water $= \dfrac{\text{loss in weight}}{\text{original weight}} \times 100\%$

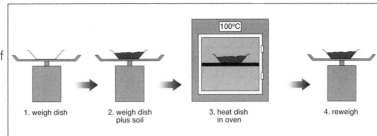

1. weigh dish
2. weigh dish plus soil
3. heat dish in oven
4. reweigh

## Finding the percentage of air in soil

1. Measure the volume of the tin (50 cm³).
2. Screw the tin into the soil. Remove a full tin of soil from the ground.
3. Fill a graduated cylinder with water up to the half-way mark (50 cm³).
4. Add the soil to the water.
5. Note the new volume (80 cm³).
6. Percentage of air $= \dfrac{\text{decrease in volume}}{\text{total volume}} = \dfrac{20 \text{ cm}^3}{100 \text{ cm}^3} \times 100\% = 20\%$

tin    soil

second volume (soil + water)

first volume (water)

## Comparing the drainage of sandy soil and clay soil

Sandy soil drains more quickly than clay soil.

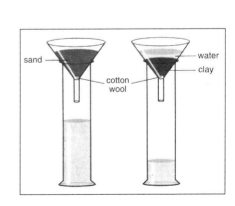

sand
water
clay
cotton wool

### Testing the pH of the soil with universal indicator paper

Test the pH of a soil sample by mixing a small sample of soil with deionised water. Most plants grow well in soil pH 6.5 - 7.0.

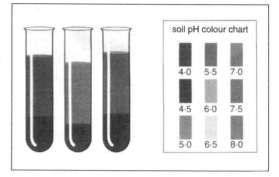

### Composts

- **Compost heaps** contain dead plants which are converted by micro-organisms into humus.
- **Sterile growing composts** are made from peat, sand, essential nutrients and vermiculite.
- **Vermiculite** absorbs water and minerals and aerates the compost.
- **Hydroponics is a method of growing plants without soil.** The plants are grown in a solution of essential elements.

## PLANT PROPAGATION

**Sexual reproduction** occurs when a male gamete from one plant fuses with a female gamete from another plant and a seed is formed. The seed germinates to produce a new plant.

**Germination** is the growth of the seed into a new plant. **Water, oxygen** and **heat** are required for germination.
Sometimes seeds may have a tough coat which prevents germination. This is called **seed dormancy**. Low winter temperatures can crack this tough coat and allow the seed to germinate.

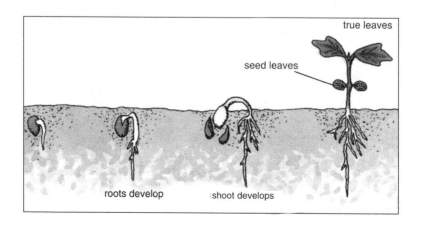

## Estimating the percentage of germination in seeds

1. Place one seed (lettuce, grass or cabbage) in each square.

2. Allow the seeds to germinate.

3. Count the number that germinate.

4. Percentage of germination =

$$\frac{\text{number of seeds that germinate}}{\text{total number of seeds}} \times 100\%$$

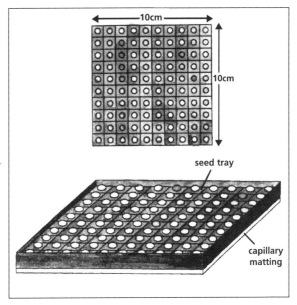

seed tray

capillary matting

## Asexual reproduction

Many plants reproduce without sexual reproduction. **No fusion of gametes** (sex cells) is involved. A sexual reproduction involves part of a plant (root, stem or leaf) growing into a new plant which is identical to the parent.

Bulbs, corms, tubers, runners and techniques using cuttings and grafting are all methods of asexual (vegetative reproduction).

## Cuttings

Cuttings are pieces of a plant (root, stem or leaves) which when planted grow into a new plant.

**Softwood cuttings** are usually taken in spring. The cutting is trimmed to just below the leaf node and the lower leaves are removed.

The cutting is then dipped in hormone powder and planted in potting compost.

**Hardwood cuttings** are taken in late autumn. A 25 cm cutting is trimmed to below the bud and the lower leaves are removed.

The cuttings are then planted in a trench about 15 cm deep with a layer of sand at the bottom.

### Grafting

Grafting is a method of plant propagation that involves inserting a bud or stem (scion) from one plant into a root or stem (stock) of another plant.

1. Select a suitable bud or stem from one plant (apple, ash or birch).

2. Insert the bud or stem into the cut surface of another plant.

3. Bind the cut surface with raffia and seal with wax. This prevents disease.

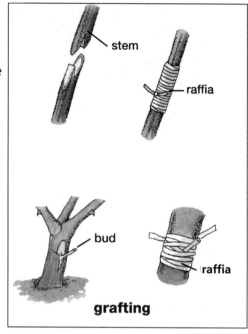

**grafting**

## GROWING PLANTS

### Factors necessary for optimum growth

- **Water:** necessary for the movement of materials during photosynthesis and respiration. The amount of water required is controlled by irrigation and by drainage. Irrigation is used to supply water to plants which do not get enough from the soil, while drainage is necessary to prevent waterlogging.
- **Nutrients:** essential for plant growth are provided by manure, compost and fertilisers.
- **Air:** necessary for photosynthesis and respiration. It contains carbon dioxide and oxygen.
- **Temperature:** Different plants need different temperatures to survive and to grow. Very high temperatures kill some plants, while frost kills others.
- **Space:** Plants need space according to their size.
- **Light:** Some plants thrive in shady conditions, while others require a lot of light.

### Growth to maturity of a vegetable

1. Germinate the seeds in a prepared seed tray.
2. Prick out the seeds when the first true leaves show.
3. Transplant the seeds to a seed box.
4. Harden off and plant out the seeds in prepared ground.
5. Water regularly and remove pests when necessary.

## Growing a pot plant

1. Transplant a geranium, or other suitable plant, into a small pot from a propagating pot.
2. Keep it in the shade and allow it to establish itself.
3. Place it in a sunny position outdoors.
4. Pinch out the growing tips of the main and side shoots. This is called **stopping**. Stopping encourages the growth of flowers.
5. Train the plant to grow into the required shape.
6. Feed the plant every 10-14 days. Do not over-water.

## Use of mulches

Mulches control moisture loss from the soil and help to control the growth of weeds. Bark, grass cuttings, compost, peat, gravel and polythene can be used as mulches.

## Grasses

The three types of grasses used in lawns are bents, fescues and ryegrass.
Bents and creeping fescues are used in ornamental lawns and golf greens. Ryegrass is a tougher grass. It is mixed with bents and fescues for use in sports-fields and common lawns.

## Cut flowers

Most flowers are harvested in the early morning.

Flowers with well-formed coloured buds which are ready to open are selected. A stem as long as possible is cut with scissors. Then the lower leaves are removed from the stem. The stems are conditioned by placing them in lukewarm water and cutting them under the water.

Adding special chemicals to the water supplies nutrients to the flowers and prevents the growth of micro-organisms.

## Diseases and pests

Fungi, bacteria and viruses are diseases that can kill plants. Potato blight is a fungus that kills potatoes. Diseases can be prevented by spraying the crop with fungicides. Plant pests include slugs, snails, caterpillars and aphids.

Plant pests are killed by insecticides and by biological control.

*Life cycle of an aphid*

Host plants

There are over 200 types of aphid in Ireland.
Black fly attacks only bean plants.
Woolly aphids live on apple trees.
There are many aphids including lettuce aphids, strawberry aphids and rosebush aphids.

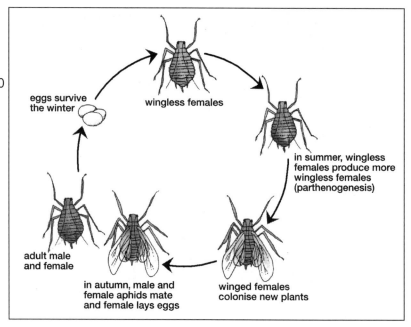

eggs survive the winter

wingless females

in summer, wingless females produce more wingless females (parthenogenesis)

adult male and female

in autumn, male and female aphids mate and female lays eggs

winged females colonise new plants

Pest control

- **Biological** control uses predators, e.g. ladybirds are beetles that eat greenfly.
- **Pheromones** are artificial hormones that lure insect pests into traps.
- **Chemical** control uses insecticides to control pests.
- **Integrated** control tries to use biological controls and limited use of chemicals to control pests.

**CHAPTER 35. MATERIALS**

# IDENTIFICATION OF MATERIALS

Materials are used in a variety of ways in everyday life. Clothes are made from different materials such as cotton, linen, wool and polyesters. Cars are made from steel, aluminium, rubber, paint, plastics and glass.

### Classification of materials

Materials can be classified into **natural materials**, such as wool, silk and cotton, or into **man-made** or **synthetic** materials, such as nylon and polythene.

Materials can also be classified according to their properties. The **main classes** are as follows:

- **Hydrocarbons** are materials that contain the elements hydrogen and carbon only. They include petrol, gas, wax, oil and tar.

- **Plastics** are man-made. Most are made from crude oil. They include polythene, PVC, teflon and terylene.
- **Textiles** are made from thin threads or fibres which are woven together. The fibres may be natural fibres like wool, silk and cotton or synthetic fibres like nylon, acrylic and polyester.
- **Metals** are usually strong and shiny and are good conductors. Some, such as silver and gold, occur free in nature while others, such as iron, aluminium and copper, have to be extracted from their ores.
- **Alloys** are mixtures of metals. They have different properties from the parent metals. Common alloys include stainless steel, brass, bronze and solder.

## USES OF MATERIALS

### Identification of different materials used for a particular purpose

| Purpose | Materials used |
|---------|----------------|
| **Buildings** | Concrete, bricks, stones, steel, wood and plastics |
| **Furniture** | Wood, plastics and glass |
| **Clothes** | Wool, silk, cotton, linen and polyesters |

### Identification of different uses of the same material

| Material | Uses |
|----------|------|
| **Steel** | Reinforcing concrete, car bodies, sinks, toilets and railway tracks |
| **Wood** | Furniture, buildings and packaging |
| **Nylon** | Carpets, clothes and containers |

### Care of materials

**Metals** corrode by reacting with air and water. Corrosion is prevented by painting, greasing, alloying, electroplating, and by galvanising and by coating with plastic.

**Timber** rots when it is untreated. Wet rot and dry rot are caused by fungi. In damp conditions the fungi multiply and feed on the wood, breaking it down. Wood is protected by painting, using preservatives, using damp-proof courses, using sealants and by proper ventilation.

**Plastics** do not corrode or rot. Some deteriorate by exposure to strong sunlight. Most plastics are **non-biodegradeable**. Biodegradeable plastics are being produced which are decomposed by micro-organisms in the soil.

**Textiles** are damaged by wear and tear, sunlight, insects and fungi. Damage to fabrics is prevented by following the instructions on the **care labels**, by fireproofing, by mothproofing and by waterproofing.

## Labelling

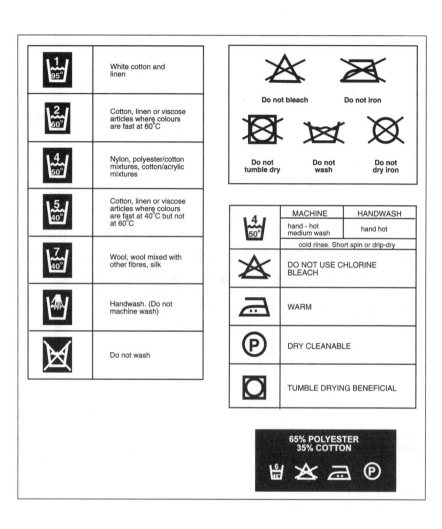

## Safety symbols

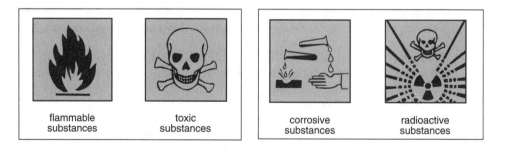

flammable substances

toxic substances

corrosive substances

radioactive substances

# PROPERTIES OF MATERIALS

The properties of <u>any one of the following materials</u> - plastics, textiles, metals or timber are studied at **ordinary level.**

The properties of <u>any two of the following materials</u> - plastics, textiles, metals or timber are studied at **higher level.**

| Material | Plastics | Textiles | Metals | Timber |
|---|---|---|---|---|
| **Origin** | Mainly from hydrocarbons | Natural and synthetic fibres | Mainly from ores; some as pure metals | Wood cut from softwood and hardwood trees |
| **Uses** | Clothes, containers and cars | Clothes and furniture | Cars and buildings | Softwood for flooring and roofing; hardwood for furniture, doors and windows |
| **Feel** | Hard and smooth | Wool is soft; nylon can be hard or soft | Cold and hard | Hard or soft |
| **Flexibility** | Flexible | Flexible | Rigid | Some rigid, some flexible |
| **Hardness** | Some hard, some soft | Usually soft | Hard | Hard or soft |
| **Density** | Varies | Varies | Usually very dense | Varies |
| **Thermal conduction** | Poor | Poor | Very good | Poor |
| **Insulating ability** | Very good | Very good | Poor | Good |
| **Flammability** | Flammable | Flammable | Non-flammable | Flammable |
| **Absorbency** | None | Good, but varies with different textiles | None | Poor |
| **Resistance to wear** | Excellent | Depends on fibres: man-made are excellent; natural are less resistant | Good | Good |
| **Reactivity** | Usually unreactive | Burn unless flame-proofed | Corrode in water and air | Rots |

## Testing the flexibility of a material (plastic, metal or wood)

1. Clamp a strip of the material to be tested.
2. Add weights to the end of the strip.
3. Measure the amount by which the strip bends on the scale.
4. Measure the amount of bending for different materials of the same length and thickness.

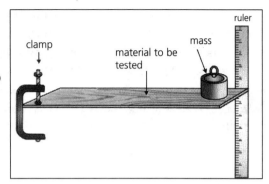

## Testing a material (plastic or metal) for hardness

1. Scratch a sample of the material with a sharp nail.
2. Repeat this test with other materials.

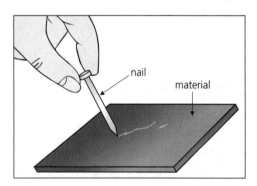

## Comparing the density of a material (plastic, wood or metal)

1. Use a balance to find the mass of the material.
2. Fill the overflow can with water until it stops dripping.

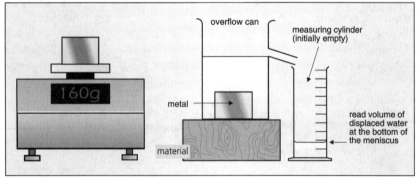

3. Place a graduated cylinder under the spout.
4. Lower the material carefully into the water.
5. Measure the volume of displaced water. This is equal to the volume of the material.
6. **Density of material** $= \dfrac{\textbf{mass}}{\textbf{volume}}$
7. Compare the density with that of other materials.

## Comparing the insulating properties of materials (plastics and textiles)

1. Fill a metal can with boiling water.
2. Measure the temperature of the water.
3. Place the can in the material to be tested.
4. Record the fall in temperature every minute.
5. Draw a graph of the fall in temperature against time.
6. Repeat the procedure for other materials.

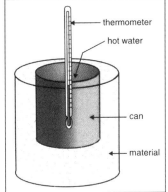
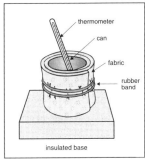

## Extracting a metal from its ore (copper from malachite)

1. Mix 2 grams of copper carbonate (malachite) with 2 grams of charcoal.
2. Wrap up the mixture in a piece of aluminium foil.
3. Heat the foil strongly for about 5 minutes.
4. Cool the contents in cold water.
5. Examine the residue for pink-brown flakes of copper.

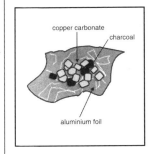
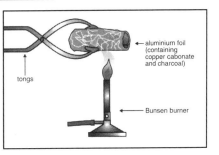

## Comparing the absorbency of different fabrics

1. Cut the fabrics to be tested into same-size pieces.
2. Find the mass of the sample.
3. Allow the sample to soak in the same amount of water for about 1 minute.
4. Remove the sample and allow it to drain for about 1 minute.
5. Reweigh the sample of fabric.
6. The increase in mass is a measure of the absorbency of the fabric.
7. Repeat the procedure for other fabrics.

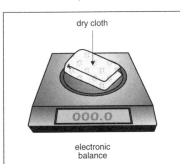
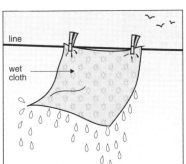
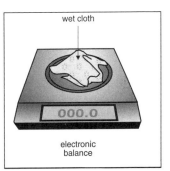

# BALANCED DIET

A balanced diet contains all the substances a body needs - carbohydrate, protein, fat, vitamins, minerals, water and fibre.

| Type | Source | Function |
|---|---|---|
| Carbohydrate | Bread, potatoes and sugar | Quick release of energy |
| Protein | Meat, fish and vegetables | Growth and repair |
| Fat | Butter, oils and margarine | Slow release of energy |
| Vitamins | Vitamin C from oranges | Healthy skin and gums |
| | Vitamin D from milk | Strong bones and teeth |
| Minerals | Calcium from milk and eggs | Strong bones and teeth |
| | Iron from spinach and liver | Makes red blood cells |
| Water | Drinks and vegetables | Prevents dehydration |
| Fibre | Cereals and vegetables | Prevents constipation |

## *Vitamins*

| Vitamin | Source | Function | Deficiency disease |
|---|---|---|---|
| Vitamin A | Carrots and fish | Healthy eyes | Night blindness |
| Vitamin B group | Liver and wheatgerm | Helps nervous system and skin | Beri beri |
| Vitamin C | Citrus fruit | Maintains healthy gums and skin | Scurvy |
| Vitamin D | Liver, fish and eggs | Forms strong bones | Rickets |

## *Minerals*

| Mineral | Source | Function |
|---|---|---|
| Calcium | Milk and cheese | Makes bones and teeth |
| Iron | Liver and meat | Makes haemoglobin in blood |
| Iodine | Sea food | Makes thyroxine in the thyroid gland |

## Food tests

| Food | Procedure | Result |
|---|---|---|
| Starch | Add iodine to food | Food turns blue-black |
| Simple sugars (glucose) | Add Benedicts solution to food, then heat gently | Solution turns green then orange |
| Proteins | Add sodium hydroxide to food<br>Add copper sulphate solution to food, then heat gently | Solution turns violet |
| Fats | Squeeze food in greaseproof paper | Translucent spot appears |

## PRESERVING FOOD

Micro-organisms spoil food by changing its taste and appearance. Preservation prevents disease and prolongs the shelf-life of food.

| Method | Procedure | Function |
|---|---|---|
| Refrigeration | Food is stored below 4 °C | Prevents growth of bacteria |
| Pasteurisation | Milk is heated to just below its boiling point and then cooled | Kills bacteria |
| Freezing | Food is stored below 18 °C | Preserves food longer by slowing down the growth of bacteria |
| Canning | Food is stored in airtight containers; bacteria are killed by adding chemicals (salt) | Prevents recontamination |
| Dehydration | Food is freeze-dried | Bacteria cannot multiply without water |
| Chemical | Salt, sugar or spices are added to food | Bacteria cannot multiply |
| Irradiation | Food is sterilised by radioactive cobalt | Food stays fresh for longer |

## FOOD ADDITIVES

Food additives are substances added to food to improve the colour, flavour and texture, and to kill bacteria.

**E-numbers** are numbers given by the European Union (EU) to particular additives.

- **Colourings (E 100 -)** are added to food to replace colour lost during cooking.
- **Preservatives (E 200 -)** slow down or kill bacteria which spoil food.
- **Anti-oxidants (E 300 -)** stop fats and oils from going rancid.
- **Emulsifiers and stabilisers (E 400 -)** emulsifiers help oil and water mix together; stabilisers prevent oil and water from separating.

### Advantages and disadvantages of E-numbers

| Advantages | Disadvantages |
|---|---|
| Preserve food | Some cause allergies |
| Prevent disease | Some may be harmful |
| Food can look and taste better | Some destroy vitamins |

## PROCESSING FOOD

### Making cheese
1. Fresh milk is pasteurised to kill bacteria.
2. Special bacteria are added to sour the milk.
3. Rennet is added to clot the milk.
4. Whey is removed from the curd.
5. The curd is salted and pressed into slabs and allowed to mature.

### Making yoghurt
1. All equipment is sterilised.
2. Dried milk is added to milk and heated above 79°C for a few minutes.
3. The milk is cooled to 43 °C.
4. Natural yoghurt is added to the milk. The mixture is poured into a thermos flask and left in a fridge for about 6 hours.

### Making butter
1. Cream is churned up in a food mixer.
2. The liquid buttermilk is drained off.
3. Salt is added to the butter to enhance the taste.

### Meat
- Pork is **cured** (by adding salt) to make bacon and ham. Curing preserves meat.
- Food is **smoked** by suspending it over a wood fire. Smoke forms a skin around the meat and seals it. Sealing prevents bacteria and oxygen from entering the meat. This preserves the meat.
- **Hormones** are used to increase the amount of meat in cattle. The EU have banned the use of growth hormones because synthetic growth hormones can build up in humans.
- **Antibiotics** are used to prevent diseases. Some farmers add antibiotics to animal feed: this is bad farming. Antibiotics from animals enter the human food chain and lessen their efficiency in humans.

### Silage

Silage is grass preserved by fermentation.

### Making silage

1. Freshly-cut grass is packed into a suitable container.
2. The container is sealed and left for fourteen days.
3. The bacteria present in the grass convert the sugar in the grass into lactic acid. Lactic acid preserves the grass.
4. Carbon dioxide is produced during fermentation.

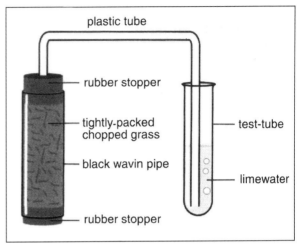

### Brewing and distilling

The brewing industry produces alcohol from sugar.

Yeast is a fungus which converts sugar into alcohol and carbon dioxide. This is called fermentation.
Distilling produces a more concentrated alcohol by removing water, e.g. wine can be converted into brandy by distillation.

### Making alcohol from sugar and yeast

1. Place some sugar in a conical flask. Add water.
2. Add some yeast.
3. Connect a conical flask to a limewater solution.
4. Carbon dioxide turns the limewater milky.
5. After some time you can smell the alcohol produced.

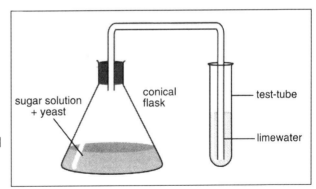

## WORLD FOOD SUPPLY

A lack of money limits the supply of food. Poor roads and war effect the distribution of food.

Famine is caused by poor rainfall, poor soil, a large population and poor technology. The effects of famine include a lack of water in the soil, poor crops and death.

# SYMBOLS

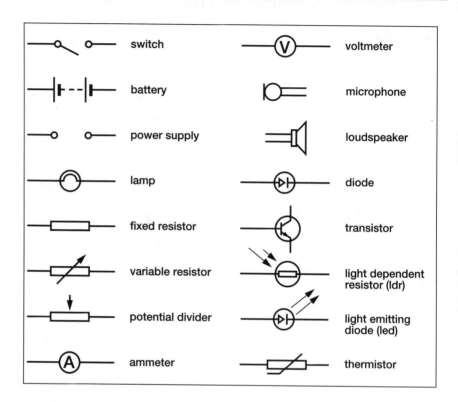

| | | | |
|---|---|---|---|
| switch | | voltmeter | |
| battery | | microphone | |
| power supply | | loudspeaker | |
| lamp | | diode | |
| fixed resistor | | transistor | |
| variable resistor | | light dependent resistor (ldr) | |
| potential divider | | light emitting diode (led) | |
| ammeter | | thermistor | |

## CIRCUITS

### Simple circuit with one switch

When the switch is closed, the circuit is complete and current flows.

When the switch is open, the circuit is not complete and no current flows.

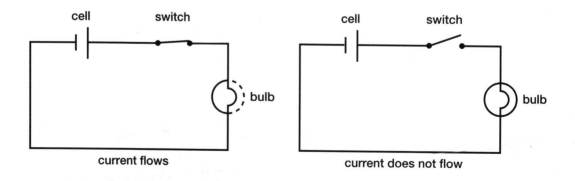

current flows          current does not flow

## Two switches in series in a circuit

The bulb lights only when A **and** B are closed.

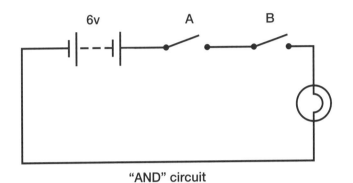

| A | B | bulb |
|---|---|---|
| open | open | off |
| closed | open | |
| open | closed | |
| closed | closed | |

truth table

"AND" circuit

## Two switches in parallel in a circuit

The bulb lights when either A **or** B is closed.

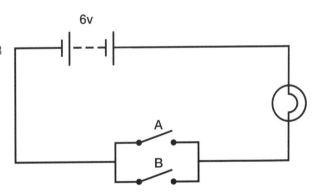

## Two-way switches

When both A and B are up the bulb lights because the circuit is complete.

When both A and B are down the bulb lights because the circuit is complete.

When one switch is up and the other is down, the bulb does not light. The circuit is not complete.

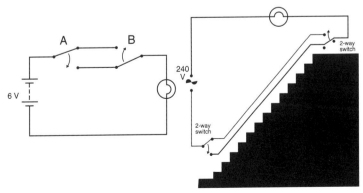

### The diode in a circuit

When the diode is in **forward bias** it has low resistance and allows current to flow. The bulb lights.

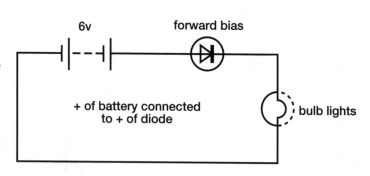

6v                    forward bias

+ of battery connected
to + of diode

bulb lights

When the diode is in **reverse bias** it has a high resistance and does not allow current to flow. The bulb does not light.

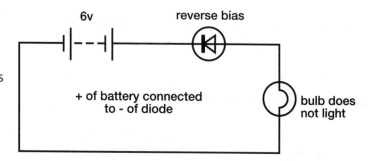

6v                    reverse bias

+ of battery connected
to - of diode

bulb does
not light

**A diode is a device which allows current to flow through in one direction only.**

### Light emitting diodes in a circuit

A light emitting diode (**LED**) is a diode that gives out light when a current flows through it. A resistor (330 Ω) is connected in series with it to prevent it from being damaged by too great a current.

LEDs are used in radios etc to indicate whether they are on or off.

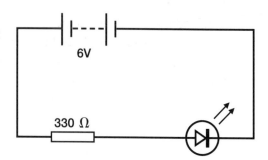

6V

330 Ω

**Light emitting diodes in a parallel circuit to check the polarity of a battery**

Two LEDs in parallel can be used to check the polarity of a battery or a power supply.

If A is the positive terminal the red LED will light because the LED is in forward bias.

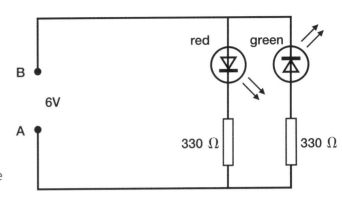

If B is the positive terminal the green LED will light because the LED is in forward bias.

## *Water-level detector*

When the water rises and touches the ends of the wires, the circuit is completed and the LED lights.

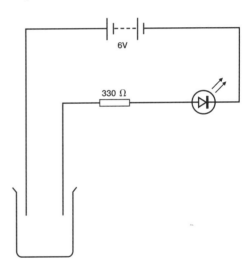

# RESISTORS

## *Variable resistor (rheostat)*

If you slide the contact to the right, the bulb dims because the resistance is increased.

If you slide the contact to the left, the bulb brightens because the resistance is decreased.

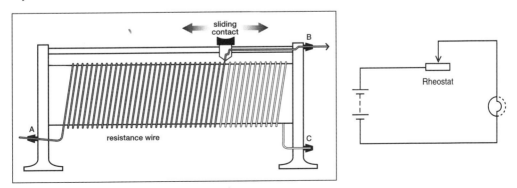

### Potentiometer

A potentiometer is a variable resistor and is used to vary the voltage produced. It can be used to control the volume on a radio and the brightness on a television set, or it can be used as a dimmer switch.

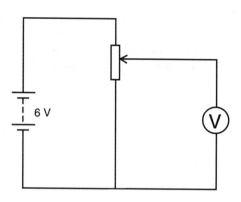

### Light dependent resistor (LDR)

An **LDR** is a resistor whose resistance changes when the amount of light falling on it changes. The resistance decreases when the amount of light increases. The resistance increases when the amount of light decreases.

LDRs are used to control street lighting, and as light meters in cameras.

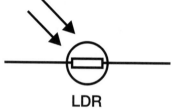

LDR

### Thermistors

When the thermistor is heated the current (and resistance) changes. A thermistor is a resistor whose resistance changes when the temperature changes. The resistance can rise or fall as the temperature increases depending on the type of thermistor.

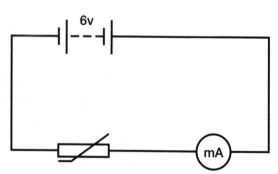

## TRANSDUCERS

A transducer is a device that converts energy from one form into another, e.g. a light bulb converts electrical energy into light energy; a loudspeaker converts electrical energy into sound energy.

## TRANSISTORS

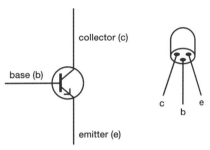

A transistor amplifies current. It converts a **tiny base current** into a much **larger current** in the **collector** circuit.

A transistor is an electronic switch that is switched on by the base current.

Transistors can be used in water-level detecting circuits and in circuits to control street lighting.

### Using a transistor as a light-controlled switch

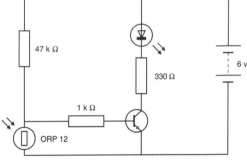

When the amount of light falling on the LDR is low, its resistance is high and very little current flows through the LDR. Instead, most of the current flows through the base of the transistor, switching it on and lighting the LED.

When the amount of light falling on the LDR is high, its resistance is low and the current flows through it and not into the base of the transistor. The transistor is switched off and the LED goes out.

Circuits like this are used to switch street lighting on and off.

### Using a transistor circuit as a water-level detector

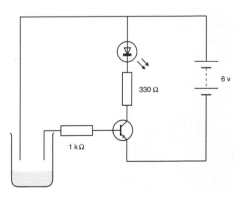

When even a tiny current flows into the base of the transistor, the current in the collector is amplified. This causes the LED to light.

This circuit can be used to show if a garden needs to be watered.

# ENERGY

**The sun is a source of all energy.**

fuels ⇐ fossils ⇐ plants ⇐ $\text{Sun}$ ⇒ plants ⇒ animals ⇒ food ⇒ humans

When something has energy it is capable of doing work.
**Energy is the ability to do work**. Energy is measured in joules (J).

## Sources of stored energy

- **Chemical energy** is stored in food, fuel and batteries.
- **Elastic potential energy** is stored in catapults and springs.
- **Gravitational potential energy** is in objects at a height because of their position.
- **Nuclei of atoms** have stored energy used in nuclear power stations and in atomic bombs.

## Sources of kinetic energy

**Moving objects** have energy which depends on their speed and on their mass. Vibrating objects transfer **sound** energy.

## Energy changes

- **Mechanical energy to heat energy:** A hammer hitting a nail produces heat.
- **Mechanical energy to sound energy:** A hammer hitting a nail produces sound.
- **Chemical energy to heat energy:** Burning a fuel produces heat.
- **Chemical energy to electrical energy to heat energy:** Chemicals in a battery produce an electric current which produces heat.
- **Electrical energy to magnetic energy to kinetic energy:** Electric energy supplied to a motor is converted into magnetic energy which causes movement.
- **Light energy to electrical energy to kinetic energy:** Energy from the sun is converted into electrical energy which can then be used to operate machines.

### Release of stored energy from food

1. Light the peanut (or any other food rich in energy).
2. The water in the test tube gets hotter.

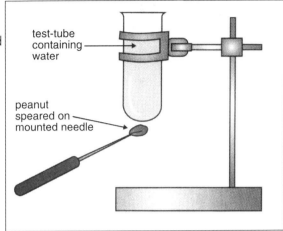

test-tube containing water

peanut speared on mounted needle

### Electromagnets

**An electromagnet consists of a coil wrapped around an iron core.**

1. When the current is switched on the nail becomes magnetised and attracts the pins.
2. When the current is switched off the nail loses its magnetism.

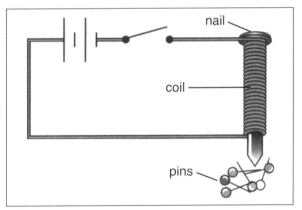

nail

coil

pins

### Electric bell

1. When the circuit is complete, a current flows and the core becomes magnetised.
   The iron armature is attracted towards the electromagnet.
2. The hammer strikes the gong and breaks the electrical circuit at the contact point.
3. The core loses its magnetism and causes the armature to move back and remake the circuit.
4. The core becomes magnetised and the cycle starts again.

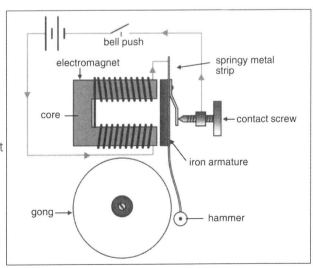

bell push

electromagnet

springy metal strip

core

contact screw

iron armature

gong

hammer

## Electric motor: electrical energy ⇒ kinetic energy

The current is switched on. It flows through the wire conductor in a magnetic field. The wire conductor experiences a force which causes the wire to rotate.

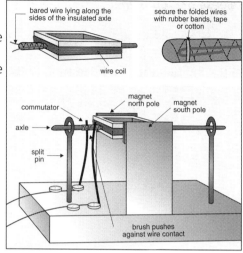

## Dynamo (generator): kinetic energy ⇒ electrical energy

1.  The magnet is moved into the coil.
2.  An electric current is induced and the needle moves to the right.
3.  If the magnet is pushed in at the other end, the needle moves to the left.

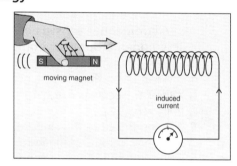

## Transformer

A transformer is a device which changes the voltage of an alternating current.

A **step-up** transformer converts a small voltage into a large voltage. This is used in television sets.

A **step-down** transformer converts a large voltage into a small voltage. This is used in transformers which convert the mains voltage into 9 volts for use in some radios.

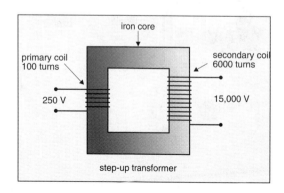

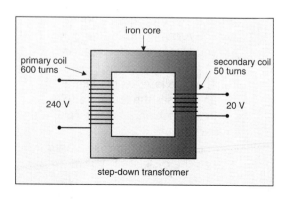

# EXAMINATION PAPERS

## JUNIOR CERTIFICATE EXAMINATION, 1997

## SCIENCE — HIGHER LEVEL

(N.B. Not for Science - Local Studies Candidates)

### TUESDAY, 17 JUNE - AFTERNOON, 2.00 - 4.30

### SECTION A (144 MARKS)
### TO BE ANSWERED BY ALL CANDIDATES
(See separate sheet for Sections B, C, D and E.)

Answer **each** of the questions, **1, 2** and **3**. There are **TEN** parts in each question. Answer any **EIGHT** parts. All questions carry equal marks. Answer the questions in the spaces provided.
Return this Section of the examination paper. Enclose it in the answer-book you use in answering the other Sections.

1.    Answer **eight** of the following, (a), (b), (c), etc.

   (*a*)   State the unit of pressure. _____

   (*b*)   The metal cube in the diagram has a mass of 72 g.

          Calculate its density

          _____

   (*c*)   What is meant by a source of renewable energy?

          _____

          Name **one** source of renewable energy. _____

   (*d*)   Give **two** advantages which a mercury thermometer has compared with an alcohol thermometer.

          (i)   _____

          (ii)  _____

   (*e*)   Complete the following.

          When the pressure on ice is increased the melting point of the ice _____.

(f)  The change of a solid directly to a gas on being heated is called _____

Name a substance which shows this property. _____

(g)  What property of light is being shown in the diagram?

_____

Which of the lines B, C or D shows
the path of the light ray from O?

_____

(h)  State how you would charge the
rod in the diagram.

_____

Suggest what happens to the pieces
of paper when the charged rod is
brought near.

_____

(i)  Name an element which can be
magnetised.

_____

What term is used to describe the two ends of a bar magnet? _____

(j)  Underline the unit of <u>energy</u> in the following list.

ampere     volt     watt     kilowatt-hour     ohm

Name another unit of energy. _____

**(8 x 6 marks)**

2.  Answer **eight** of the following, (a), (b), (c), etc.

(a)  Give **a** difference between a solid and a liquid.

_____

(b)  Name both of the compounds whose chemical formulae are given below.

| Formula | Name |
|---------|------|
| $NH_3$ | |
| $H_2SO_4$ | |

(c) The diagram shows apparatus which may be used to remove permanent hardness from water.

  (i) Name substance A.

  _____

  (ii) Give **one** cause of permanent hardness in water.

  _____

Water
A

(d) Sketch the electronic structure of an atom of calcium. (See Mathematics Tables, pg 44.)

(e) Balance the following chemical equation.

$$H2O2 › H2O + O2$$

Name a catalyst for the reaction. _____

(f) What is meant by electrolysis? _____

_____

_____

(g) What treatment of water

  (i) kills micro-organisms? _____

  (ii) prevents tooth decay? _____

(h) What is meant by oxidation? _____

Underline the substance oxidised in the reaction:

$$Zn + Cu^{++} › Zn^{++} + Cu$$

(i) State **two** methods by which corrosion of metals may be prevented.

  (i) _____

  (ii) _____

(j) Name

  (i) an element that is a liquid at room temperature. _____

  (ii) an element that is stored in oil. _____

**(8 x 6 marks)**

3.  Answer **eight** of the following, (a), (b), (c), etc.

    (a)  State **two** characteristics of living organisms.

        (i) _____

        (ii) _____

    (b)  The diagram shows a microscope.

        Name part A.

        _____

        What is the function of part B?

        _____

        _____

        _____

    (c)  Blood vessels carrying blood away from the heart are called

        _____

    (d)  Name the type of joint found at the hip. _____

        What is the function of cartilage in a joint? _____

        _____

    (e)  Name an endocrine gland in the human body. _____

        What hormone does this gland release? _____

    (f)  What will be observed to happen to
        the limewater in this test tube after an
        interval of time?                                         Woodlice

        _____

        Give a reason for this.                                              Limewater

        _____

    (g)  Give an example of the use of micro-organisms in medicine. _____

        _____

142

(h) Name the process occurring in the diagram.

_____

Where in the human female reproductive system
does the process shown usually occur?

_____

Ovum

Sperm

(i) Underline the human characteristics in the following list which are usually inherited.

     accent     eye colour     length of fingernails     shape of ear lobes

(j) Give **two** features of a flower which help in pollination by insects.

(i) _____

(ii) _____

**(8 x 6 marks)**

## SECTION B,C,D,E

These sections should be answered in your answer-book. Answer **ONE** question from each of the **Sections B, C and D**. All questions carry equal marks. Answer **TWO** questions from **Section E**. All questions carry equal marks.

### SECTION B — PHYSICS (48 marks)

Answer **either** question **4** or question **5**.

4. (a) Name an instrument used

(i) to measure the length of a curved line;

(ii) to measure the diameter of a copper pipe     (6)

Describe how you would use the instrument in (i) above to calculate the length of a river on a map.     (9)

Explain how the instrument in (ii) above could be used to measure the thickness of the copper in the copper pipe shown in the diagram.     (9)

Copper

(b) State the law of the lever.     (3)

Describe an experiment to verify the law of the lever.     (9)

Give two examples of levers.     (6)

The centre of gravity of the metre rule shown in the diagram is at the 50 cm mark. The metre rule is balanced under the forces shown.

Calculate the **position** of the 4 N force. (6)

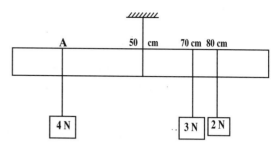

5. (a) What is meant by convection? (3)

Draw a diagram of an apparatus used to show convection in a liquid. Label your diagram. (9)

You are given three metal rods made of aluminium, brass and copper respectively. They are each of the same length and diameter as shown in the diagram.

Outline a laboratory experiment to show which metal is the best conductor of heat. (9)

In cold winter weather birds often fluff up their feathers. Explain how this helps the birds to keep warm. (3)

(b) What is meant by the **frequency** of a wave? (6)

Give an example to show that sound travels more slowly than light. (3)

Describe, using a labelled diagram, an experiment to demonstrate that sound does not travel through a vacuum. (9)

Standing in front of a cliff face, a boy shouts and 4 seconds later he hears an echo of his voice. If the speed of sound is 340 metres per second, calculate the boy's distance from the cliff. (6)

### SECTION C — CHEMISTRY (48 marks)

Answer **either** question **6** or question **7**.

6. (a) State two differences between a mixture and a compound. (6)

You are given a mixture of sulphur and iron filings.

(i) What colour would you expect the mixture to be? (3)

(ii) How would you separate the mixture of sulphur and iron filings? (3)

Name another method of separating a mixture. (3)

The diagram shows the mixture of iron filings and sulphur being heated. Write a chemical equation for the reaction which takes place in the test tube. Name the compound which is formed as a result of the reaction of iron and sulphur. (6)

Give a precaution which should be taken when heating a test-tube in the laboratory. (3)

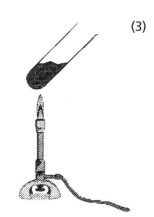

(b) The diagram shows the items of apparatus which could be used in an experiment to prepare a salt.

(i) Name the items of apparatus labelled C and D. (6)

(ii) Name a salt which could be prepared using this apparatus. (3)

(iii) Name the two substances which would be used to prepare this salt. (6)

(iv) State the term used to describe this type of reaction. (3)

(v) How would you make sure that you accurately read the level of the liquid in C? (3)

(vi) What is the function of an indicator in this experiment? (3)

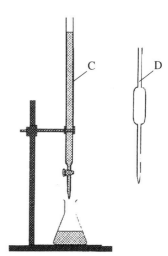

7. (a) Arrange the following metals in order of **increasing** reactivity:

iron         silver         sodium         calcium         (6)

The diagram shows one of the above metals in water.

(i) Name the metal. (3)

(ii) Write an equation for the reaction of the metal with water. (3)

Which one of the metals above does **not** react with dilute hydrochloric acid? (3)

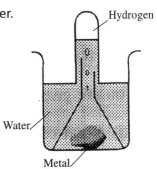

State how you would test the oxides of the four metals above to see whether they are acidic or basic. In the case of any **two** of the metals above state the result you would expect to obtain. (9)

(b)

| I | | | | | | | | O |
|---|---|---|---|---|---|---|---|---|
| 1 | | | | | | | | 2 |
| **H** | | | | | | | | **He** |
| Hydrogen | | | | | | | | Helium |
| 1 | **II** | | **III** | **IV** | **V** | **VI** | **VII** | 4 |

| 3 | 4 | | 5 | 6 | 7 | 8 | 9 | 10 |
|---|---|---|---|---|---|---|---|---|
| **Li** | **Be** | | **B** | **C** | **N** | **O** | **F** | **Ne** |
| Lithium | Beryllium | | Boron | Carbon | Nitrogen | Oxygen | Fluorine | Neon |
| 7 | 9 | | 11 | 12 | 14 | 16 | 19 | 20 |

| 11 | 12 | | 13 | 14 | 15 | 16 | 17 | 18 |
|---|---|---|---|---|---|---|---|---|
| **Na** | **Mg** | | **Al** | **Si** | **P** | **S** | **Cl** | **Ar** |
| Sodium | Magnesium | | Aluminium | Silicon | Phosphorus | Sulphur | Chlorine | Argon |
| 23 | 24 | | 27 | 28 | 31 | 32 | 35 | 40 |

| 19 | 20 |
|---|---|
| **K** | **Ca** |
| Potassium | Calcium |
| 39 | 40 |

The diagram shows part of the Periodic Table of the Elements. Study the diagram and answer the following questions.

(i) Name the group of elements in each case, the atoms of which

   (a) have a full outer electron shell; (3)

   (b) have 7 electrons in their outer shell. (3)

(ii) Name an element which generally forms ions with a charge of +2. Explain why this happens. (6)

(iii) Name an element which generally forms ions with a charge of -1. Explain why this happens. (6)

(iv) What information is given by the number above each atomic symbol? (3)

(v) What information is given by the number below each atomic symbol? (3)

## SECTION D — BIOLOGY (48 marks)

Answer **either** question **8** or question **9**.

8. (a) State the function of the lungs. (3)

The diagram shows a human lung.

Name the parts labelled Y and Z. (6)

State the function of Y. (3)

Explain what happens at Z. (6)

Name an animal which does not have
lungs. (3)

How does the animal which you have
named receive its oxygen? (3)

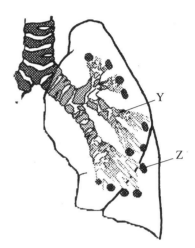

(b) State the term used to describe the response of a plant (i) to gravity, (ii)
to light. (6)

Describe, using a labelled diagram, an experiment to show the response
of a plant to gravity. (9)

How does a plant benefit from its response to gravity? (6)

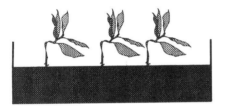 

The diagram shows two Petri dishes containing green cress plants. Suggest a
reason why the plants in A are not upright as in B. (3)

9. (a) the diagram shows the structure of a canine tooth.

Name the parts labelled A and B. What is the
principal function of a canine tooth? (9)

How do teeth help in the digestion of food? (3)

Name any **two** of the stages of human nutrition
other than digestion. (6)

State what happens during **each** of the stages
you name. (6)

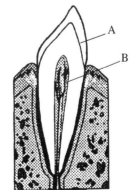

(b)  Give **two** causes of soil pollution. (6)

Leaching is more likely to occur in sandy soil than in loamy soil.

(i)  What is leaching? (3)

(ii)  How does leaching affect the soil? (3)

Describe, using a labelled diagram, an experiment you would carry out to measure the amount of air in a soil sample. (12)

## SECTION B — APPLIED SCIENCE (72 marks)

Answer **TWO** questions from this section.

10. **EARTH SCIENCE.** Answer any **two** of the following, (a), (b), (c).

(a)  Describe the solar system with the aid of a diagram. (12)

What is a galaxy? Give an example of a galaxy. (6)

(b)  Explain the terms (i) evaporation, (ii) condensation. (6)

Describe how clouds are formed. (6)

Name a type of cloud and state the kind of weather which you would expect to have with this type of cloud. (6)

(c)  State Charles' law. (6)

The apparatus shown in the diagram was used in a laboratory experiment to verify Charles' law.

What will you observe happening as the beaker of water is heated? (3)

Explain how the apparatus could be used to verify Charles' law. (9)

11. **HORTICULTURE.** Answer any **two** of the following, (a), (b), (c).

(a)  Name **two** methods for the vegetative (asexual) propagation of plants. (6)

Give an advantage of vegetative propagation of plants. (3)

Describe how you would carry out vegetative propagation using one of the methods you have given above. (9)

(b)  Explain the following terms in relation to growing plants from seeds:
(i)  dormancy
(ii)  germination
(iii)  pricking out
(9)

State **three** conditions which are necessary for the successful germination of a seed. (9)

(c) Name **two** nutrients essential for healthy plant growth. (6)

Describe an experiment to show how a lack of one of the nutrients you have named affects plant growth. (6)

What are the components of a potting compost? (6)

12. **MATERIALS SCIENCE**. Answer both parts.

(a) The following are types of material commonly used in manufacturing.

           plastics        metals

  (i) In the case of each of the above materials name a product which can be manufactured from it. (6)

  (ii) State why each of the materials is suitable for the use indicated in (i) above. (6)

State how (i) timber, (ii) fabric, may be protected. (6)

(b) Identify each of the following hazard symbols. (6)

A                        B

Describe, with the aid of a diagram, how you would carry out one of the following experiments.

  (i) To compare the insulation properties of two different plastics.

  (ii) To demonstrate the extraction of a metal from its ore.

  (iii) To compare the absorbency of two different types of fabrics.

  (iv) To compare the bending strengths of two woods. (12)

13. **FOOD**. Answer any **two** of the following, (a), (b), (c).

(a) State a function of carbohydrate in the human diet. (3)

Name the elements present in a carbohydrate molecule. (6)

Describe a laboratory experiment to test a food sample for glucose. (6)

Name **one** other food type. (3)

(b) What is the purpose of pasteurisation? (3)

Describe how milk is pasteurised. (6)

Pasteurised milk is used to make cheese.

Give the other steps involved in the production of cheese. (9)

(c) What is silage? (3)

Give an advantage of silage over hay as feed for animals. (3)

Describe, using a diagram, a laboratory experiment to make silage. (12)

14. **ELECTRONICS**. Answer both parts.

(a) Name the components labelled A and B in the diagram. (6)

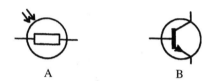

Study the circuit diagram and answer the following questions.

(i) What are the items labelled X and Y? (3)

(ii) What will happen (a) to X and (b) to Y when the circuit is switched on? (6)

(iii) Explain your answer in (ii). (3)

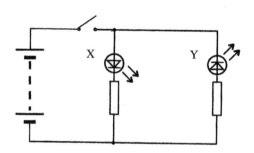

(b) Name and give the function of the meters S and T in the circuit diagram. (12)

What is the function of R? (3)

How does R work? (3)

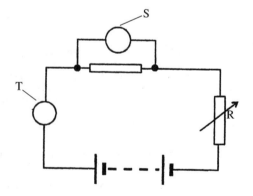

15. **ENERGY CONVERSIONS**. Answer both parts.

(a)  What is nuclear energy?  (3)

State an energy change that occurs in each of the following.

  (i)  Water is being released from a dam.

  (ii)  A nuclear power station is in operation.

  (iii)  An electric motor is running.  (9)

Explain, using a diagram, how you would make a simple electric motor.  (9)

(b)  The diagram shows a transformer.

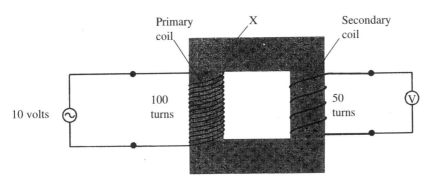

Name the part labelled X.  (3)

The primary coil in the transformer is connected to a 10 volt a.c. supply as shown. What reading would you get on the voltmeter connected to the secondary coil?  (6)

Name the type of transformer shown in the diagram.  (3)

Give an example of the use of a transformer in the home.  (3)

## JUNIOR CERTIFICATE EXAMINATION, 1996

# SCIENCE — HIGHER LEVEL

(N.B. Not for Science — Local Studies Candidates)

TUESDAY, JUNE 11 — AFTERNOON 2.00 - 4.30

**SECTION A** (144 marks) **TO BE ANSWERED BY ALL CANDIDATES.**

(See separate sheet for Sections B, C, D, E)

Answer **each** of the questions 1, 2 and 3. There are **TEN** parts in each question. Answer any **EIGHT** parts. All questions carry equal marks. Answer the questions in the spaces provided.

Return this Section of the examination paper. Enclose it in the answer-book you use in answering the other Sections.

1. Answer **eight** of the following, (a), (b), (c) etc.

   (a) The densities of mercury, lead and gold are 13.6 g cm$^{-3}$, 11.3 g cm$^{-3}$ and 19.3 g cm$^{-3}$ respectively. What will happen when (i) a piece of lead, (ii) a piece of gold, is placed in a beaker of mercury?

   (i) _____  (ii) _____

   (b) A car starts from rest with a constant acceleration of 6 m s$^{-2}$. How long will it take to reach a speed of 30 m s$^{-1}$? _____

   (c) What is meant by the term biomass? _____

   Give an example of biomass. _____

   (d) Underline the two renewable energy sources in the following list:

   oil, wind, gas, coal, hydroelectric.

(e) The diagram shows a uniform lever suspended at its mid-point which is balanced under the action of two weights as shown.

20 cm       30 cm

X       6N

Calculate the moment of the 6 N weight.

_____

Calculate the value of the weight X.

_____

(f) What is the main way in which heat is transferred when

   (i) the water in an electric kettle is heated? _____

   (ii) the Sun heats the Earth? _____

(g) Give a reason why water is not a suitable liquid for use in thermometers.

_____

_____

(h) State the effect of increased pressure on

   (i) the boiling point of water. _____

   (ii) the melting point of ice. _____

(i) Name the object shown in the diagram.

_____

Give a common use for this object.

_____

brass

iron

(j) The diagram shows a periscope.

Complete the path of **one** of the two light rays from the object to the eye of the observer.

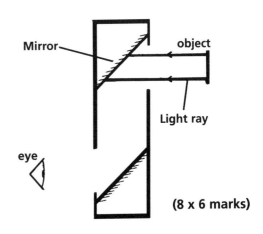

Mirror

object

Light ray

eye

**(8 x 6 marks)**

2. Answer **eight** of the following (a), (b), (c) etc.

(a) An atom is made up of a _____ surrounded by _____

(b) Name one mixture in each case that may be separated by

   (i) filtration. _____

   (ii) distillation. _____

(c) In an exothermic reaction heat is _____

   An example of an exothermic reaction is _____

(d) Iron filings are observed to increase in mass after rusting.

   Explain this observation. _____

   _____

(e) State **two** of the requirements for a fire to continue burning.

   1. _____

   2. _____

(f) Complete and balance the following equation.

$$Mg + HCl \longrightarrow$$

(g) Name the piece of glassware shown in the diagram.

   _____

   What is the purpose of the mark on the stem?

   _____

**Mark**

25 cm³

(h) Name **a** gas which dissolves in rainwater to form acid rain. _____

   What harm is caused by acid rain? _____

   _____

(i) Give an effect of hardness in water. _____

   How may temporary hardness in water be removed? _____

   _____

*(j)* The diagram shows a dry cell.

Name the substances X and Y.

X _____

Y _____

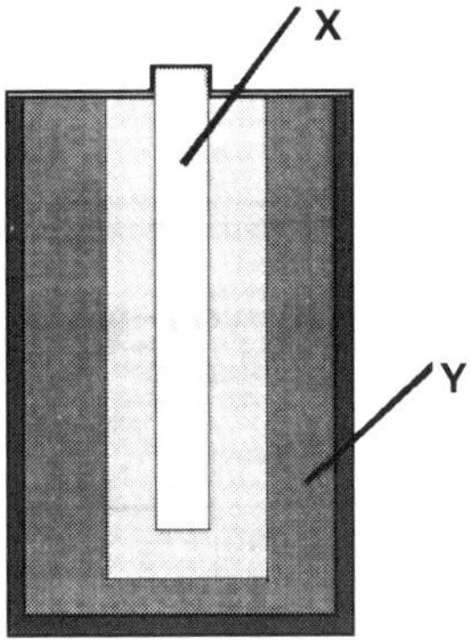

**(8 x 6 marks)**

3. Answer **eight** of the following *(a)*, *(b)*, *(c)* etc.

*(a)* The diagram shows a plant cell.

Name the parts labelled X and Y.

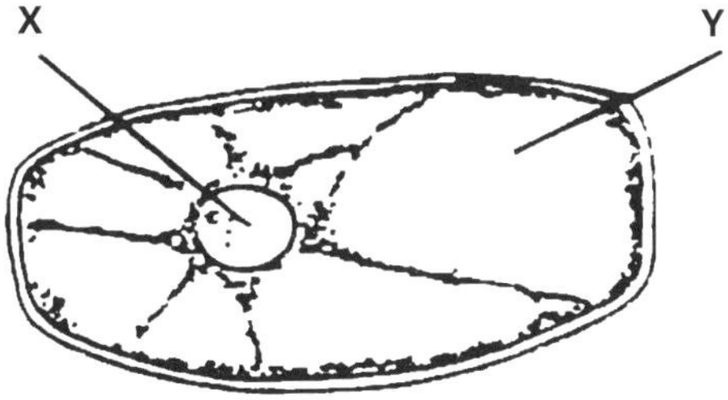

X _____

Y _____

*(b)* What is meant by geotropism? _____

_____

How does geotropism affect the shoot of the plant? _____

*(c)* The five stages of human nutrition are

ingestion, digestion, absorption, assimilation and egestion.

Explain the underlined terms.

digestion _____

assimilation _____

*(d)* Name a chamber of the human heart. _____

Give the function of the part of the heart you have named. _____

_____

*(e)* Name one part of blood. _____

State the function carried out by the part of the blood which you have named._____

_____

(f) State two locations in the human body where there is a synovial joint.

(i) _____

(ii) _____

(g) Name an endocrine gland in the human body. _____

Name a hormone released by the gland which you have named. _____

_____

(h) Name the piece of apparatus, shown in the diagram, which is used in fieldwork.

_____

State the use you would make of the apparatus.

_____

_____

(i) Water moves through the stem of a plant in tissue called _____ and food

moves in tissue called _____.

(j) In order for photosynthesis to occur _____ and

_____must be present.

**(8 x 6 marks)**

AN ROINN OIDEACHAIS

# JUNIOR CERTIFICATE EXAMINATION, 1996

# SCIENCE — HIGHER LEVEL

(N.B. Not for Science — Local Studies Candidates)

TUESDAY, JUNE 11 — AFTERNOON 2.00 - 4.30

### SECTION A

Section A is on a separate sheet which provides spaces for your answers.
The completed sheet should be enclosed in your answer-book.

### SECTIONS B, C, D, E

These sections should be answered in your answer-book.
Answer **ONE** question from each of the **Sections B, C, and D**. All questions carry equal marks.
Answer **TWO** questions from Section E. All questions carry equal marks.

## SECTION B — PHYSICS (48 MARKS)

Answer **either** question 4 **or** question 5.

4. *(a)* What is meant by the centre of gravity of a body? (3)

Describe how you would determine the centre of gravity of a sheet of plywood. (9)

Explain why the centre of gravity of a double decker bus should be as low as possible? (6)

*(b)* What is meant by weight?

Calculate the weight of an object of mass 10 kg. ($g = 10$ m s$^{-2}$) (6)

The object was then moved to the Moon, where the value of the acceleration due to gravity, g, is one-sixth of the Earth's. What is now (i) the mass, (ii) the weight, of the object? (6)

*(c)* Define pressure. State the unit in which pressure is measured. (9)

A cube of side length 2 metres as shown in the diagram has a mass of 16 kg. If the cube is lying with one face on the ground, calculate the pressure exerted by the cube on the ground. ($g = 10$ m s$^{-2}$). (6)

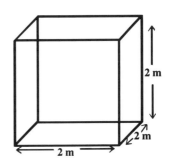

Why is the water storage of a house usually situated in the attic? (3)

5. (a) State Ohm's law.

The circuit shown was used in an experiment to verify Ohm's law.

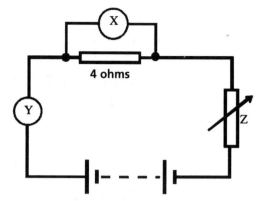

4 ohms

(i) Name the meter X. (3)

(ii) State the measurements which should have been taken during the experiment. (6)

(iii) What would you expect the reading on meter X to be when the reading on meter Y is 1.5? (6)

(iv) State the function of the part Z. (3)

Sketch the graph which you would expect to obtain from the experiment. (6)

(b) The diagram shows part of an E.S.B. bill for electricity used in a house.

| Meter Readings | | Units and Rate | | Amount |
| Present | Previous | (pence) | Description | (CR = Credit) |
|---|---|---|---|---|
| 53233 | 52427 | N x 7.14 | General Domestic | 57.55 |
| | | | Standing Charge | 6.60 |
| | | | Special Discount | 3.05 CR |
| | | VAT @ 12.5% on | £61.10 | 7.64 |
| | ................. | ........................... | ...................... | ................. |
| | Electricity | Charges this | period | 68.74 |

(i) What is the scientific term for the unit used by the E.S.B. in its bills? (3)

(ii) Calculate from the E.S.B. bill above the number of units, N, of electricity used. (3)

(c) What is meant by the power rating of an appliance? (3)

Name

(i) a domestic appliance which has a low power rating;

(ii) a domestic appliance which has a high power rating. (3)

State the function of a fuse. Give an example of an appliance which would require a 3 ampere fuse. (6)

## Section C — Chemistry (48 marks)

Answer **either** question 6 **or** question 7.

6. (a) Define atomic number. (3)

State the group number in the Periodic Table of (i) the alkali metals, (ii) the halogens. (3)

Name one alkali metal and one halogen. (3)

Describe how you would examine the reaction of the alkali metal, which you have named, with water. Give the equation for the reaction. (9)

State the type of bond which is formed between the alkali metal you named and the halogen you named. Show with the aid of a sketch how the bond is formed. (6)

(b) What is a fuel?

Explain how fossil fuels are formed. (9)

The products of the reaction which occurs when natural gas ($CH_4$) is burned are carbon dioxide and water.

Describe a chemical test you would perform to show that a particular colourless liquid is water. (6)

Draw a labelled diagram of the apparatus you would use to prepare carbon dioxide in the laboratory. (6)

Give two everyday uses of carbon dioxide. (3)

7. (a) Diagram (i) shows the apparatus used in the electrolysis of water.

State a substance from which the electrodes could be made. (3)

Name A and B. (6)

What information does this experiment give about the composition of water? (3)

What substance must be added to the water so that a current will pass? (3)

What will be observed to occur when a current is passed in the circuit shown in diagram (ii)? Explain your observation. (6)

Give an industrial use for this type of process. (3)

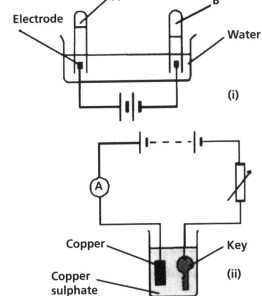

159

(*b*) What is (i) an acid, (ii) a base? (6)

Name and give the chemical formula of (i) an acid and (ii) a base. (6)

Give a balanced chemical equation for the reaction between the acid and the base which you have named. (3)

What is this type of reaction called? (3)

Sketch the apparatus which you would use when carrying out this experiment accurately in the laboratory. (6)

## Section D — Biology (48 marks)

Answer **either** question 8 **or** question 9.

8.  (*a*) Carbon dioxide and urine are among the substances excreted by the human body.

The diagram shows the urinary system in the human.

Identify and give the function of each of the parts labelled X, Y and Z. (12)

Name the organ through which carbon dioxide is excreted.

Describe an experiment to compare the amount of carbon dioxide in exhaled air and in inhaled air (12)

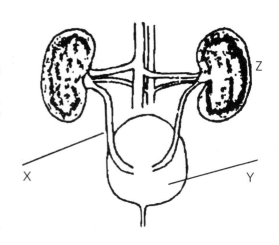

(*b*) Explain the terms (i) sensory nerve, (ii) motor nerve. (6)

A person accidentally touches a hot surface with the hand and the hand is rapidly withdrawn. Explain how the sensory and motor nerves acted to protect the person from a severe burn. (6)

The diagram shows the eye.

Name the parts labelled A and B (6)

Give the function of the part labelled C. (3)

Where is the blind spot of the eye? (3)

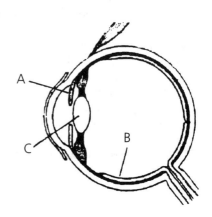

9. (a) What is meant by sexual reproduction?

Describe how sexual reproduction occurs in the flowering plant. (12)

The diagram shows a flower.

Name the parts labelled A and B.

State the function of each part. (12)

(b) Name two plants and two animals from a habitat which you have studied.

Select one of the plants and one of the animals which you have named and explain how each has adapted to its habitat. (12)

Give a food chain (with three members) from the habitat. (3)

Describe a laboratory experiment to measure the percentage of air in a soil sample. (9)

## Section E — Applied Science (72 marks)

Answer **TWO** questions from this Section.

10. **EARTH SCIENCE**. Answer any **two** of the following, (a), (b), (c).

(a) The Earth and the Sun are part of the Solar System which is in the galaxy called the Milky Way.

(i) State two differences between the Earth and the Sun. (3)

(ii) Describe briefly the Milky Way galaxy. (6)

(iii) Outline the life cycle of a star. (9)

(b) The Moon orbits the Earth and it is the major influence on our tides. During the month the Moon, as seen from the Earth, changes in appearance. These changes are called the phases of the Moon.

(i) Explain how the Moon influences tides on the Earth. (9)

(ii) Why does the Moon's appearance change during the course of each month? (6)

(iii) What causes a lunar eclipse? (3)

(c) (i) Because of the greenhouse effect the Earth is sufficiently warm to support life as we know it. What causes the greenhouse effect? (6)

(ii) List three measurements which are made by meteorologists in recording and forecasting the weather. Name the instrument used in each case. (6)

(iii) Explain how clouds are formed. (6)

11. **HORTICULTURE**. Answer any **two** of the following, (a), (b), (c).

    (a)  What is meant by grafting?

          Give an advantage of grafting. (9)

          Describe, using a diagram, how grafting may be carried out. (9)

    (b)  Name three grasses found in lawn seed mixtures. (6)

          Name a grass which must be included in a seed mixture for

          (i)  a football pitch;

          (ii)  a golfing green?

          Give a reason for your choice in each case. (9)

          Give an identifying characteristic of **one** of the grasses which you named. (3)

    (c)  Name two common garden insect pests. (3)

          Describe the life cycle of **one** of the insects which you have named. (12)

          Explain how you would control this insect in the garden. (3)

12. **MATERIALS SCIENCE**. Answer **both** parts.

    (a)  Name (i) a natural textile, (ii) a synthetic textile. Give an example of a textile which is a mixture of natural and synthetic fibres. State an advantage of this textile. (9)

          Sketch a care symbol commonly found on clothing and state what the symbol means. (6)

    (b)  Answer **one** of the following.

          (i) **PLASTICS**
          Name two common plastics. (6)

          Describe an experiment to compare the densities of the two plastics. (15)

          (ii) **METALS**
          Name a commonly used metal and the ore from which it is extracted. (6)

          Describe an experiment to compare the flexibility of two named metals. (15)

          (iii) **TIMBER**
          Name **one** hardwood and **one** softwood. (6)

          Describe an experiment to show the effect of grain direction on the strength of a piece of timber. (15)

13. **FOOD**. Answer any **two** of the following, (a), (b), (c).

(a)    (i) What is a protein? (3)

(ii) Give the function of protein in the diet. (3)

(iii) Give two sources of protein. (3)

(iv) Describe how you would carry out a laboratory test to show the presence of protein in a food. (9)

(b)  What is meant by (i) curing, (ii), smoking, meat? (6)

State the basic principles involved in (i) the curing, (ii) the smoking, of meat. (6)

Indicate the undesirable side-effects of **either** hormones **or** antibiotics when used in food production. (6)

(c)  Describe an experiment to compare what happens to (i) cooked food, (ii) uncooked food, which is exposed to the air. (9)

Explain how food is preserved by dehydration. (6)

What is meant by an anti-oxidant? (3)

14. **ELECTRONIC**S. Answer **each** part.

(a)  The circuit shown contains a switch S.

Name the device X. (3)

What term is used to describe the way X is arranged in the circuit? (3)

State what you would observe when switch S is closed. (3)

Give another use which can be made of X. (3)

(b)  State the function of the potentiometer in the circuit shown below. (3)

State what happens to the lamp as the contact Z moves towards X.

Explain your answer. (6)

(c)  What is a transducer?
Name **two** electrical transducers. (9)

Give the circuit symbol for (i) a transistor, (ii)  a light dependent resistor (LDR). (6)

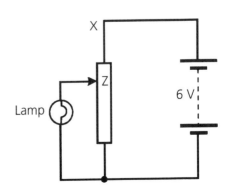

15. **ENERGY CONVERSIONS**. Answer **both** parts.

(a) What is meant by kinetic energy? (3)

Name a device, one in each case, in which the following energy conversions take place

    (i)   chemical energy to electrical energy;

    (ii)   electrical energy to kinetic energy;

    (iii)   kinetic energy to heat energy. (9)

State an energy conversion which takes place in the light bulb. (3)

(b) The diagram shows a circuit containing a coil and a galvanometer.

Describe what is observed as the magnet is moved into the coil. Explain your answer. (6)

Name a device which is based on the principle being demonstrated here. (3)

Outline how the device you have named operates. (12)

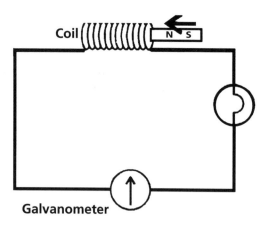